PRAISE FOR *FORCE OF NATURE*

"Gisèle Huff tells a powerful story about tragedy, perseverance, and empathy for our fellow humans. Reading this book will undoubtedly help prepare you for life's challenges and successes. I count myself among the many people Gisèle has inspired throughout her life. Her drive to push America toward adopting a universal basic income has been important to me and is a reason why this idea was and remains so vital."

—**Andrew Yang**, 2020 Democrat presidential candidate and author of *The War on Normal People*

"Beyond any doubt, Gisèle Huff has lived a life of real purpose and meaning. *Force of Nature* describes her life story, which is full of passion and grace. Among her many accomplishments, Gisèle's advocacy for customizing students' learning experiences will be long lasting."

—**Jeb Bush**, former governor of Florida

"Gisèle Huff's life is indeed remarkable—and then some. Her vision and laser focus on transforming K–12 education moved major philanthropists to realize the critical role that technology plays in making education joyful and supporting all learners in realizing their goals. An early supporter of the Khan Academy, Gisèle serves as a constant inspiration for the work we do here. She was always there to help me believe in myself and what we needed to do to help hundreds of millions of learners around the world."

—**Sal Khan**, founder and CEO of Khan Academy and author of *The One World Schoolhouse: Education Reimagined*

"When anyone loses every male member of her family in the Holocaust and then her husband and son to cancer, and still summons the courage to fight for a better world, I pay close attention. Gisèle Huff's journey is a lesson in how to embrace every day with passion, generosity, and grace. This book will change you."

—**Sue Toigo**, founder of the Toigo Foundation

"It's a rare moment when the title of a book captures the essence of its author. Gisèle Huff, a Holocaust survivor and immigrant who first fled and now fights injustice, is a true force of nature. Fearless, with the courage to speak truth to power, Gisèle displays a passion and honesty that has built bridges and incubated new ideas for our country. Whether pursuing disruptive innovation in improving education for all children or offering solutions to the potentially devastating job displacement from the forthcoming technological revolution, Gisèle is relentless and tireless. After facing a series of heartbreaking tragedies, she offers personal insight and lessons on how to survive and persevere. An insightful read from a true mensch."

—**Andy Stern**, president emeritus of SEIU and author of *Raising the Floor: How a Universal Basic Income Can Renew Our Economy and Rebuild the American Dream*

"I know first-hand that Gisèle Huff is, in fact, a force of nature. Her story of perseverance, growth, and generosity is inspiring. Through it all she has demonstrated her commitment to the power of education and to the priority of meeting individual students' needs and preparing them for lives of purpose and promise. Our enduring relationship and my deep respect for Gisèle prove that mutual trust can indeed make it possible to work through ideological barriers to reach a shared aspirational vision."

—**Becky Pringle**, president, National Education Association

"Any conversation with Gisèle Huff results in a positive whirl of disruption, challenge, and inspiration. All achievers can see around corners; Gisèle is one of those rare doers who removes whole structures that have long held us back. There are many conversations in this book—struggle, joy, anguish, accomplishment, hope—that speak to us as individuals and as a nation at a transformative time. Most importantly, this book provides the opportunity to engage with a remarkable person who constantly forces each of us to examine the present to envision the future."

—**Bob Wise**, former governor of West Virginia

"Gisèle Huff's memoir is an engaging delight to read, filled with wisdom drawn from more than eight decades of exuberant life. The arc of the story starts as her family flees Nazi-occupied France and ends with an admonition against the resurgence of racism and antisemitism in America. In between is the story of her profoundly human-centered work in education, technology, and the universal basic income movement. Hers is also a deeply human story. Even in the face of profound loss, Gisèle summons an optimistic, hopeful, and determined framework for life. Her contributions and her indomitable spirit have made her a legend in the not-for-profit world."

—**Katherine Bradley**, founder and chair of CityBridge

"Gisèle Huff takes us on her amazing journey through her survival of the Holocaust, during which time her life was disrupted by evil, and her years devoted to positive, innovative disruption for the benefit of humanity. Not often are we privileged to share in the intimate details of a life that begins in Nazi-occupied France, then, through dedication and brilliance, effectively pursues national education reform here in America before inspiring the top social, economic, and political titans of our millennium to tackle the future shock of economic displacement with the guaranteed income remedies for which she has become a force of nature."

—**Dave Cortese**, California state senator

"Gisèle's life is one directed by recognition of people's humanity, a solid basis for a life spent as a bridge builder. The impulse to connect and listen is how we met, and these pages detail her evolving inquiry into a world of connection. This beautiful book tells the story of struggle, growth, and the process of a life well lived."

—**john a. powell**, director of Othering and Belonging Institute and professor of law, African American studies, and ethnic studies at the University of California, Berkeley

"She's not just a Holocaust survivor. As Gisèle details in this tour de force of her life and impact, she's a thriver who has helped transform minds, conversations, and lives—including mine. The embodiment of the American dream resides in these pages."

—**Michael B. Horn**, author of *From Reopen to Reinvent: (Re)Creating School for Every Child*

"Towards the end of this incredible book of an incredible life put to words (which I blew through in one five-hour sitting), Gisèle Huff writes, 'I am a survivor because life is the most precious of all things, and what you do with it is the reason you are living it.' If there's one thing I hope readers walk away with from this book, it is that every human being deserves the opportunity to fulfill their full potential as empowered individuals and members of their communities, at as small a scale as the family to the larger scale of the nation to the largest scale of the entire human race. No one alive today does anything entirely on their own, and none of us would be where we are today without those who came before us—and those like Gisèle who do everything they can in the present to make a positive difference in this world, who truly believe in the torch of hope and hold it aloft to light the way for others. When Gisèle writes that the concept of universal basic income 'just happens to be the last, best hope for the human species,' know that these words come from someone who knows better than most living today just how bad things can get, and how great things can be, if we just set sail for a new world that we together—and only together—have the power to reach."

—**Scott Santens**, UBI advocate and author of *Let There Be Money*

"Gisèle's riveting life is one of love, loss, and the persistence needed to make the world a better place. Her story spans eight decades and includes firsthand experiences of some of the most harrowing moments in history. Her intellectual and political evolution is a particularly important narrative in this moment of seemingly entrenched polarization."

—**Natalie Foster**, cofounder of the Economic Security Project

Force of Nature

Force of Nature

The Remarkable True Story of One Holocaust Survivor's Resilience, Tenacity, and Purpose

GISÈLE HUFF

Published by Simonet Press, San Francisco

Cover design: Megan Katsanevakis
Project management: Devon Fredericksen and Mari Kesselring
Editorial production: Abi Pollokoff

ISBN (paperback): 979-8-9864234-0-1
ISBN (e-book): 979-8-9864234-1-8
ISBN (audiobook): 979-8-9864234-2-5

Think big, start small, move fast.

—Gerald Huff

CONTENTS

PART III

PROLOGUE

I love America. If it weren't for the American armed forces liberating France from the Nazi occupation in 1945, I wouldn't be here to tell you my incredible story. The American liberation of France allowed me to immigrate and become the person I am, a skeptical optimist who is as persistent as a dog with a bone and as disruptive as a rock in a pond. Throughout my eighty-six years, I've faced dreadful challenges due to both the circumstances in which I found myself and the personal grief I had to endure. Although I was never interned in a concentration camp, I lost eighteen members of my family to the Holocaust. When I was eleven, my mother and I immigrated to America with our hearts full of hope and only $400 to our name.

Despite my impoverished and terrifying early childhood, I've achieved remarkable success in America. I'm not speaking of financial success. I'm speaking of the success of making an impact and contributing to the betterment of my fellow human beings. As my friend and onetime colleague Bob Wise, the former governor of West Virginia, wrote, "Gisèle Huff lives a phenomenal life consistently devoted to directly inspiring more people to achieve more positive social impact than anyone I have ever met."

Hope sustained me through terrible hardship and led me to find meaningful purpose in life. Because education was my path to the American Dream, I devoted my career to making sure education was available to every child in this nation. Part I of this book describes my childhood in war-torn France, making my way to the United States, and launching a twenty-two-year-long career focused on improving kindergarten through grade-twelve education. My aim in sharing the challenges and great loss I faced during this period is to show that as long as there is life, there is hope. I have come to understand that when hope is matched with purpose, the results are tremendous.

I've also come to understand that we can achieve so much by joining forces and collaborating. Some of my greatest successes resulted when I set aside my assumptions about people and focused on our common goals. As you'll see in part II of the book, although I didn't succeed in my run for Congress when I was sixty years old, it was through this experience that I met people from both sides of the aisle committed to improving the K–12 education system. For over two decades I worked alongside these incredible minds, fueled by the hope that together we could make a difference, because ultimately, a well-educated populace is the lifeblood of democracy. During this time, I met and engaged with many disparate people: former governor Jeb Bush (R); former governor Bob Wise (D); the late John Walton, member of the Walmart family; Senator Cory Booker; Charles Koch, leader of Koch Industries; and Reed Hastings, co-founder of Netflix. Collaborating with people of diverse ideological backgrounds enabled me to accomplish so much over my career.

While I was working in education, the world around me was changing at a rapid pace. I had long believed in the American Dream, which asserts that anyone can succeed if they work hard enough. I considered myself a Libertarian; I favored minimal state intervention in the free market and in the private lives of citizens. But as you'll see in part III of the book, my mind changed when my son, Gerald, introduced me to the concept of a universal basic income (UBI), which rests on the same principles as learner-centered education, in which children are given tools to take charge of their own education as they get older. With UBI, citizens share the prosperity that they helped create by receiving income with no strings attached. At first, I resisted the idea of UBI. But Gerald's research changed my mind. Who would have thought that I, a dedicated believer in the power of the free market, would eventually head a foundation devoted to ensuring every citizen receives a basic income? I've learned that there is so much power in changing your mind. No matter how attached a person is to their ideas, anyone can change and grow just as I did—all it requires is an open mind.

Immigrating to America after having lived through the horrors of the arbitrary rule of France by an evil foreign power made me particularly aware of the privileges that democracy bestows. This is why I've voted in every election and an important reason why I ran for Congress in the 1990s. This is also why, in my later years, I have tried to give back by working for causes that seek to improve the country that I love.

I hope you'll enjoy reading about my journey. It's my wish that you'll see how hope, collaboration, and an open mind helped me achieve all that I have. And I ardently wish that the two big ideas that fueled my journey, the transformation of K–12 education and the rewriting of the social contract that binds us as a country, will resonate with you as well.

Part 1

CHAPTER 1

I was born on June 23, 1936, on a stormy night in Paris, to a working-class family of Russian Jewish immigrants. My maternal grandparents escaped Ukraine at the beginning of the First World War so that my grandfather, who was a teenager at the time, could avoid being drafted in the tzar's army. My paternal grandfather, a middle manager at a jam factory in Odesa, fled with his wife and five children in 1922 to escape the Bolshevik revolution.

My mother was born in Paris and my father was seventeen years old when he arrived. They met at a dance hall in the early 1930s. At that time, dance halls were the hub of the social lives of the young working class. My mother was an excellent dancer and every weekend she went to the local ballroom. It's there that my aunt introduced her to my father. He looked like Rudolph Valentino, the silent-screen heartthrob. Although my father was eight years older than my mother, the age difference wasn't an issue. Having grown up in Paris, my mother was very sophisticated and well educated. They consistently won dance contests, the tango being their specialty. They married in February 1934, two years before my birth.

They moved into the same building where my maternal grandparents lived and left me in their care when my mother went back to work as a secretary. My father was a bookbinder and worked with my grandfather. My grandmother did not speak French, and the first word I spoke as a baby was "*zeide,*" the Yiddish word for *grandfather.*

We had a three-room flat in a building in a dead-end alley: a living-dining room heated by a wood-burning stove, a bedroom, and a kitchen. The water closet contained just a toilet (considered a luxury because many of the buildings in the neighborhood only had public toilets at each landing), and my parents went to a public bath house once a week to bathe. I was washed in the sink.

In 1940, when I was four years old, the Germans occupied France after launching what was dubbed the *blitzkrieg.* My father was drafted in 1939 to serve in the French army, and he participated in the failed attempt to stop the Germans from invading France. Tragically, the French generals used outdated strategies to fight the battle. They put their faith in the Maginot Line, concentrating their entire force on the border between France and Germany. The Germans first invaded Belgium and then easily went around the Maginot Line, entering France from the north. Over a period of six weeks, from May 10 to June 25, 1940, Hitler's armies defeated France and its allies, driving them westward to the debacle of Dunkirk.

In early June, as the Germans swept through the countries to the north, three-quarters of Parisians fled the city in what became known as "the Exodus" because it harked back in scope to biblical times. My mother was working for a very prosperous international engineering firm headquartered in

Switzerland. The firm organized a convoy of cars to extract its employees from Paris. On our way out of the city, I found myself sitting on the lap of the CEO. I don't remember much of the journey except a vague recollection of getting carsick. Paris was declared an open city on June 13, 1940, and the French government surrendered on June 22. I turned four years old the next day. We evacuated to Pau, where the firm put us up in a hotel, and we didn't return to Paris until the end of June. My mother and I were lucky to have survived the Exodus because, as people clogged the roads to escape from the advancing troops, the Germans strafed the columns of refugees and many were killed.

When we made our way back to Paris, we reunited with my father, who had been released from his military service when the French army was disbanded. We found the city under the total control of the Germans, and under their rule, Jews were required to register at their local police station because the Hitler regime had embarked on a genocidal campaign they termed "the Final Solution." Our identity and ration cards were stamped with the word *"JUIF"* in red. We were forced to sew a six-pointed yellow star with *"Juif"* stitched in black onto all of our clothing. Because we lived in a predominantly Jewish neighborhood, it did not seem odd to me to wear the yellow star, because everyone else around me wore it, too. It was only outside of my neighborhood that I felt the stigma of being visibly marked by the yellow star. Despite these terrifying circumstances, everyday life resumed under the Occupation. My father went back to his job as a bookbinder, and my mother went back to work as a secretary for the Swiss engineering firm. My maternal grandparents continued to provide day care for me.

Even decades later, it's difficult to understand how an entire free people could carry on day-to-day life under these horrific circumstances. But humans are exceptionally adaptable and soon grow accustomed to what Hannah Arendt, a German Jewish philosopher, coined "the banality of evil." We went about our business, dutifully registering at city hall and sewing the symbol of our persecution onto our clothing. We had no idea what the Germans had imposed on other countries they had conquered, so in the summer of 1940, we were not terribly apprehensive about the future. Of course, I was a child, so I really didn't know how the adults felt, but for me, life resumed as it had before the Occupation.

In August 1941, the Nazis arrested my father, my uncle, and my grandfather. The raid was prompted by the killing of German soldiers in our working-class neighborhood, where Communist sympathies were very strong. The partisan attack on the Germans marked the beginning of the French resistance movement. Branded by the Jewish star and tracked through their registration at the police station, my father, uncle, and grandfather were rounded up on the street and at home. I remember my grandmother, my mother, and I hiding in the back room of the bar across the alley from our apartment during the raid. I needed to go to the bathroom and had to squat in a corner of the room because there was no access to a toilet. By this time, we were well aware of the potential danger we were in, but there was very little that working-class people without the means to leave France could do.

We were terrified, not knowing where the men had been taken or if they'd return. My grandfather was released because the Nazis were still promoting the myth that they sent Jews to labor camps, and he was too old for the work. My father and uncle were incarcerated in Drancy, the infamous holding camp outside of Paris, for seven months until March 1942, when they were in the first convoy of deportees transported to Auschwitz. They were murdered there a few months later.

The Germans were very clever in their propaganda. They played on the French population's chauvinism and, in addition to the labor-camp myth, they invented a repatriation myth that purported to send foreign Jews back to their countries of origin. Most French people were either indifferent to or in agreement with this policy. The French police made arrests based on lists maintained by French bureaucrats. Many French citizens denounced their Jewish neighbors out of spite or for personal gain.

In 1942, the Nazis set out in earnest to rid France of its Jewish population. Over a two-day raid in July, they arrested 13,152 foreign-born Jewish men, women, and children and held them in a sports venue, the Vélodrome d'Hiver, until they were loaded in cattle cars and sent to Auschwitz. My grandparents were part of that raid and did not survive the transport to the concentration camp. Nor did my father's two sisters, their husbands and their four children, my grandmother's cousin, her husband and daughter, or my second cousin's mother and father. One of my uncles managed to survive incarceration until after D-Day in 1944 but was killed on a death march from one concentration camp to another. Because my mother and I were French born, we were spared deportation.

Looking back on that period, what I remember most is how scared I felt all the time. No one knew what happened to those who were deported, and I clung to my mother, both of us bereft of our familial support system. It was especially traumatic for my mother. She was brought up in the tight-knit, insular Russian Jewish community in Paris, a shy, diffident woman deeply immersed in family life. In the space of less than a year, those closest to her disappeared. Had I not been with her, she might well have given up. But the last thing her parents said to her was "Take care of Gisèle," and she wouldn't give up on me. At the time, she was twenty-six years old.

By the winter of 1942, we began hearing rumors that unspeakable fates awaited those taken away by the Nazis. Because my mother was French born, the Nazis hadn't gotten around to arresting her yet. But we no longer believed that being born in France would protect us from deportation. When alerts came of impending raids, my mother and I would flee our apartment and spend the night in the offices of her firm. At one point, desperate to save my life, she decided to take me to live with a non-Jewish family outside of Paris. But when she tried to leave me at their home, I made such a scene that she couldn't go through with it. It turned out that this decision saved both our lives, and looking back on that episode, I'm astounded that despite being an obedient child I found the voice that changed the course of events. If I hadn't hysterically demanded that she not leave me, she would not have taken the drastic and extremely difficult steps to escape Paris and go into hiding with me.

Remembering her state of mind in that awful winter of 1942, my mother said, "I asked myself, 'What am I doing here waiting in my apartment like a sitting duck for them to come and get me and my daughter?' Something told me 'Run, run, run.' And I did." What a radical departure this was from her nature. It speaks volumes about maternal and survival instincts and her hope for a better future for me. Too many Jews waited until it was too late and were trapped.

CHAPTER 2

Leaving Paris presented two major problems: where to go and how to get there. Our identity papers forbade any kind of travel. My second cousin had found refuge with a friend of hers who had two young daughters and was hiding in a small town in the southwest of France. My mother decided that our best option was to make our way there. At least she would have a support system in place. But there was still the problem of our unusable identity papers. She got in touch with my father's best friend, who was himself in hiding in Paris. He had a connection to the French Underground. Through him she secured a false identity card using her own first name, Berthe, and the last name of a woman whose records had been destroyed, Simonet. In March 1943, Berthe Simonet and her daughter, Gisèle, set off on a train journey fraught with danger from Paris to Toulouse, where we boarded a bus to Salies-du-Salat, a small town about forty-five miles from Toulouse known for its mineralized water spa.

On that long, terrifying ride, my mother drummed into my head that I could never reveal that we were Jewish. In fact, given my age, she explained that I had to enroll in the local Catholic church to study the catechism in preparation for my first communion. I complained bitterly to my mother that I didn't want to go because praying hurt my knees, but she told me we had no choice and that I should always remember who I really was.

On the day after our arrival, our friend's daughters and I went down to the town plaza after dinner. The girls were both around my age, and as we played ball, a teenager came up to us and asked who I was. "She's our cousin from Paris," one of them replied. "Then you must be Jewish, too," she said, and I said, "Yes." This was an automatic, thoughtless response from a seven-year-old, but I was petrified, convinced that we were doomed. I ran upstairs to my mother, crying, "Someone knows we're Jewish!" Thankfully nothing came of it because the girl whom I told was Jewish herself.

In Salies-du-Salat my mother had no means of income; there were no jobs in that small town for an accomplished secretary who had worked at a big international firm in Paris. Ever resourceful, she came up with a solution. She bought a rickety old bicycle and rode through the hills to farms to purchase fruits and eggs. She then packed them in a suitcase and took them to Toulouse to sell on the black market. Although the countryside was somewhat safe from the confiscations and requisitions of the Germans, Toulouse was not as protected, and the foodstuffs my mother sold were in high demand. Black marketing was punishable by death, and if the Germans discovered the contents of her suitcase, she would have been shot on the spot. But she had no choice. After she had pawned her engagement and wedding rings, she had had nothing left, so she took the risk.

When she traveled to Toulouse, she was away for days at a time. To keep me safe, she boarded me on a farm where my assigned jobs were either to sit on the geese while they were force-fed to produce foie gras or to mind the sheep in the fields. Accompanied by a dog who did all the work, I kept an eye on the herd, although in retrospect, I don't know what I could have done about keeping the sheep safe since I was only eight years old.

It was a major culture shock for a city girl like me to live on a farm, with the farmer, his wife, and their two burly sons. I don't remember much from that time except being in a field and losing one of my knitting needles, one of my few possessions. I desperately looked for it to no avail. I was devastated. I also vividly remember the delicious taste of goose fat–slathered peasant bread baked at the farm.

For two years my mother and I managed to survive undetected. My last memory of Salies-du-Salat is watching out of the window of our one-room flat as defeated German soldiers streamed past. Still very fearful of the German army, everyone in town stayed indoors, and I remember my mother and I expressing disbelief that the war was really over. Living in hiding, fearing that my mother would get caught and I would never see her again made me old beyond my years. Essentially, I never had a childhood. I can't even remember what happened before the Germans invaded France. Up to the age of nine, I lived in a nightmare that felt like it would never end. I lost eighteen members of my family, including my father. That is why I will be forever grateful to America for having liberated us.

Although decades have passed, I still get emotional when I think of that harrowing time. In 1999, I visited the United States Holocaust Memorial Museum in Washington, DC, and just as I was about to leave the building, emotionally drained from the horrors it depicted, I saw a sign pointing to the archives. The Nazis were meticulous in their record-keeping, and the museum is one of the repositories for the lists they kept. The signs led to a library-like setting. I approached the woman at the desk and asked whether the library held information on French deportees. I gave the librarian the names of my immediate family members, and she confirmed that my father and uncle had both died in Auschwitz in the summer of 1942. She also confirmed that my grandparents died on the train to Auschwitz in 1942. I cannot describe how I felt reading the names Gregoire Sledowker, Adolphe Kogan, and Mira and Benjamin Kogan. Seeing their names on a printed page—a ledger of death—devastated me. The other times in my life when I experienced the same feeling were when I admitted to being Jewish on my second day in Salies-du-Salat, and more than forty years later, when the doctor told me that my husband was terminally ill with pancreatic cancer.

Nothing can ever convey the magnitude of the loss of six million Jews, but I will forever be grateful for the memorials to the victims of the Holocaust—how they uphold the motto "Never Forget." I've visited the Mémorial de la Shoah (Holocaust Museum) in Paris, where the names of my family members are inscribed into the concrete wall. I've also visited Yad Vashem in Jerusalem, the World Holocaust Remembrance Center, an impressive monument to all those who perished and an archive of the horrors of the Holocaust. As I walked through the room where French Jews were memorialized, I could not stop crying. I had the same reaction when I watched the movie *Schindler's List*. At the end of that black-and-white film, when the Jews saved by Schindler place a stone on his grave, the film captures the tradition in vivid color. I sobbed in the movie theater long after it emptied. Although I am not an observant Jew, my connection to the history of my people is extremely strong. Being Jewish is much more than a religion; it carries the weight of having been persecuted for millennia.

CHAPTER 3

When the war ended in 1945, my mother and I couldn't wait to return to our apartment in Paris. My aunt had continued to pay rent on the flat in hopes that we'd safely return. My father's youngest sister, Sarah; my paternal grandmother; and my cousin, Henry, had managed to survive in Paris. My grandmother never left her one-room apartment for the duration of the war. My aunt lived at the bakery where she worked, and she brought supplies to my grandmother when she could. My cousin hid with his paternal grandparents in a Parisian suburb, where they lived off the land and received occasional help from one of their sons. They were spared because they hadn't registered, and they hid in locations that weren't on the Germans' rosters.

It was not easy to evade the Nazis. For example, my father's friend Theodore and his wife lived in a nice neighborhood with their two young daughters and their housekeeper. When the Occupation began, he and his wife made a big show of departing their house with several suitcases in hand, leaving their daughters and the housekeeper behind. They snuck back in under the cover of darkness and never left the house until Paris was liberated. Their French housekeeper had to shop for food at several different markets so that no one would suspect that two additional adults lived there. She took their daughters to school and ostensibly raised them, a ruse that saved four lives.

As you can imagine, the end of the war was chaotic for all the displaced survivors. Family members made frantic efforts to find their kin and help them. Luckily, we had family outside of France. When my father's family escaped to Paris from Odesa in 1922, they had sent their eldest son, Milton, to New York to facilitate their immigration to the United States. However, when Congress passed the Immigration Act of 1924, it drastically curtailed immigration.

To illustrate how difficult it was to immigrate, I include below a quote from the History, Art & Archives of the House of Representatives about that act:

> On this date, the House passed the 1924 Immigration Act—a measure which was a legislative expression of the xenophobia, particularly towards eastern and southern European immigrants, that swept America in the decade of the 1920s. Authored by Representative Albert Johnson of Washington (Chairman of the House Immigration Committee), the bill passed with broad support from western and southern Representatives, by a vote of 323 to 71. "It has become necessary that the United States cease to become an asylum," Representative Johnson declared during debate on the bill. Among its provisions, the act created a permanent quota system based

> on "national origin." It limited the number of immigrants that could be admitted to the US to two percent of the total number of individuals from each nationality that resided in the United States in 1890—before waves of Slavic and Italian immigrants arrived in America. Despite vigorous protests from Japanese diplomats, the measure also excluded Japanese immigrants (a ban that would not be lifted until 1952). Finally, it allowed no more than 150,000 total immigrants who fell within the parameters of the quota system to enter the US in any one year. After Senate passage, the Immigration Act was signed into law in late May 1924.

Since many of the Jews persecuted by the Nazis were from the Slavic countries, this act effectively shut the door on people like my father's family. Worse still, in May 1939, after the Kristallnacht pogrom six months earlier had made clear to the world that the Nazis were implementing onerous persecutions of German Jews, the US refused entry to some nine hundred of them on the *St. Louis*, a ship that sailed from Hamburg, Germany, to Havana, Cuba, on their way to America. The passengers were told they needed to obtain visas as required by the act, and they could not disembark in Cuba. They had to return to Europe, and almost a third of them subsequently died in the genocide.

After the war, my uncle Milton located what remained of his family and sponsored his mother, sister, and nephew to come to America. As soon as my aunt arrived in 1946, she enlisted our extended family members in New York to sponsor my mother and me. In June 1947, we boarded a converted

Liberty ship that had been used for troop transport during the war, departing from Le Havre. When we crossed the channel and reached Southampton, I was amazed to hear the dock workers speak English, a language I thought only European elites spoke. For ten days we slept in forty-eight-bed, women-only dorms and ate cafeteria style. Luckily, I didn't get seasick, a problem that afflicted most of the passengers. That meant I was one of a handful to partake in the abundant food on offer in the cafeteria, a drastically different experience from the near starvation of my entire childhood. I reveled in the pleasure of eating foods like bacon (which I had never seen before) and bananas (which I hadn't eaten in years).

In the early morning of September 21, 1947, we sailed by the Statue of Liberty in New York Harbor. We understood too well her motto of "Give me your tired, your poor, your huddled masses yearning to be free . . ." I will never forget the feeling of hope that swelled in my chest as I stood on the deck at sunrise with the statue towering over me. I wish I could capture for you my reaction to seeing that iconic statue after living through a five-year nightmare that seemed it would never end.

CHAPTER 4

When we arrived in New York, we had only what we could pack into our suitcases and $400 to our name. Neither of us spoke English, other than a few standard sentences we had learned from a French–English dictionary. When we disembarked, we found New York in deep mourning because legendary mayor Fiorello La Guardia had died the day before. But despite the somber mood, the sights and sounds overwhelmed me. The city was so much bigger than Paris. Because it hadn't suffered any damage during the war, the streets and buildings radiated prosperity, buoyancy, and hope. My first visit to a supermarket was an Alice in Wonderland experience: I had never seen such abundance in my entire life. I could not remember having encountered an orange, and here were hundreds of them displayed in a brilliantly lit setting. I couldn't believe my eyes.

My mother and I moved in with my aunt, grandmother, and cousin. They lived in a ground-floor one-bedroom tenement apartment in the South Bronx. As I look back on our living arrangements, I marvel at how adaptable human beings are and how strong family ties can be. My grandmother and my aunt slept together in the bedroom, my mother slept on the living room sofa, and my cousin Henry and I slept head to toe on a rollaway bed.

My cousin Henry, who is six months older than I am, arrived in New York a year before I did. He still lives in New York and speaks unaccented English, whereas I retain the trace of a European accent. I can't explain why that is; there was no difference in the way we assimilated. When I think about it, Henry is the only person left in the world who knew me when I was a child. He helped introduce me to life in New York, and I remember that on New Year's Eve 1948, we went by ourselves to Times Square to watch the ball drop. I was eleven and a half and Henry was twelve. We took the subway from the Bronx. Of course, this is unimaginable now, but even as late as 1972, my eight-year-old son took two buses by himself to get to his school on the other side of Manhattan.

The tenement where we lived was in a predominantly Black neighborhood in the South Bronx. During my childhood in France, I had seen no more than a dozen Black people on the streets of Paris. Of course, we all knew of Josephine Baker, the iconoclastic performer who reigned over the city's musical scene, but until I arrived in the South Bronx, I had had no contact whatsoever with Black people. I entered PS 2, my neighborhood school, as a sixth grader. The school was dubbed "the city zoo" and was housed in a crumbling building that had been a hospital during the Civil War. I was one of three white students among my thirty or so Black classmates. I spoke no English, so the culture shock was exacerbated by the fact that I didn't understand anything said in the classroom.

My first day of school in New York I walked into the old, dilapidated building to a classroom filled with boisterous sixth graders, more than 90 percent of whom were Black. I had always attended all-girls schools, so being in a classroom with boys was just as foreign to me as the English everyone spoke. The classroom was dingy with high ceilings and little light. The teacher was a young Jewish woman who had the look of a deer caught in the headlights. She didn't seem to have a lesson plan, valiantly trying to keep order while my classmates read comic books and bounced Spalding balls against the wall. I didn't know what to make of the situation. My schooling in Paris was demanding and formal. We wore smocks, we stood when an adult entered the room, and we never said a word out of turn without being punished. Although it was a public school in a country where the separation between church and state was rigorously enforced, it operated like a parochial school without the nuns. So imagine my shock finding myself at PS 2. I thought I had landed in *The Snake Pit*, a popular movie at that time about a woman who finds herself in an insane asylum and can't remember how she got there. In the most progressive city in America, in 1947, Black kids were being warehoused and no one was learning anything in that dismal classroom. My education came to a standstill, which is a shame because before we left for America, I was awarded the Prix d'Excellence at my school in Paris, the highest recognition given for academic performance. The prize was a large hardcover book, a translation into French of *A Tale of Two Cities*, illustrated with still shots from the American movie. It graces the shelf of my bookcase to this day.

After three weeks of my coming home crying because I wasn't learning anything, my mother took her French–English dictionary in hand and went to speak to the assistant principal. When she gingerly complained about the lack of academic rigor, he told her, "Madam, we believe it is more important that we teach children how to get along with each other," which wasn't happening, either. Later, when I began working in education, my mother and I would reminisce about this episode, one that underscored for me how long children of color have been shortchanged in this country.

Thanks to the teachers that took an interest in me, I learned English and survived ten months at PS 2. My teachers encouraged me to take the test for the Hunter College Elementary School, a highly competitive institution founded in 1940 for Manhattan's gifted children. Unfortunately, my grasp of English was not good enough for me to gain admission. It wasn't my first missed opportunity for advanced education. In June 1947, just before we left southwestern France for Paris, a national committee selected me to attend a school that trained low-income children to become teachers. I was an excellent student and would have thrived at such a school. But my mother had to make the agonizing choice to forgo the opportunity so we could move to the United States. I wasn't the only one to sacrifice, either. My mother was in a serious relationship with a man who had been convicted of operating on the black market, which made him ineligible to immigrate to the United States. But because she hoped for a better future for me, she had to leave him behind. Just as her instincts prompted her to leave Paris when she did, she instinctually knew that I had a much better chance for a good life in the United States. That was the best decision she ever made. Had we stayed in France, I would never have made myself into what I am today. The circumstances would not have allowed it. In New York in the 1940s, the American Dream was still achievable, allowing for upward mobility through hard work and dedication, especially if you were white and had access to a good education. At that time, the gap between the haves and have-nots was narrower, and *what you did* rather than *who you knew* was a much better determinant of what you could achieve than it is now. Meanwhile, European countries clung to the class system that kept people relegated to the stations they were born into.

My mother found work as a secretary in a French company where she learned English on the job. We moved out of the South Bronx within a year and rented a studio apartment on West Eighty-Fourth Street, a walk-up one-room efficiency with a closet that had been transformed into a kitchen. We had an icebox, which was literally a box with shelves on the bottom and a compartment on top to hold a block of ice to keep food fresh. I'll always remember how the Italian man who delivered the ice every week hit on my mother, an attractive, blond Frenchwoman. It's funny how certain inconsequential scenes live on in memory.

After our move, I attended Joan of Arc Junior High School, a good neighborhood school where I perfected my English and followed the traditional middle-school curriculum. As I remember, most of the children were white. I have no recollection of making any friends or having playdates. My life was totally entwined with my mother, and I entertained myself with the radio, the occasional movie, and books. Because of the rigorous curriculum in my French schools, I was much more academically advanced than my classmates. Despite having just learned English, I was at least a year ahead of them. My experience at PS 2 in the South Bronx and at Joan of Arc Junior High in Manhattan gave me a unique perspective on how different education is for students living in low-income neighborhoods. This was the beginning of my interest in addressing educational disparity between races and socio-economic classes.

Today, many of the people engaged in the bloody battles over school reform, especially as it affects low-income children, don't understand the fundamental problem already visible in the late '40s. The public-school system in America is neither rigorous enough nor personalized enough to prepare children to do more than fit as cogs in a postwar industrialized society. However, it was designed in such a way that it could also nurture the 15 percent of those who later assumed leadership roles and brought on the prosperity of the '50s and the innovations of the '80s and onward—one of the reasons why America became the most successful country in the world in the mid-twentieth century. America was also one of the few participating western nations that hadn't been devastated by World War II. Another reason America flourished is that in America, innovators are allowed to fail. Other industrialized countries attach a cultural stigma to failure that precludes innovators from trying again—and again. Think about how remarkable it is that Americans elected a president in 2016 who billed himself as the world's best dealmaker, yet he had experienced numerous business failures.

In 1950, when she was thirty-four years old, friends introduced my mother to Sol Baron, a widower who went by his Russian name, Zunia. She went on to marry Zunia, with the hope that my stepfather could provide more opportunities for me—once again, making a decision for my benefit. Even though he was twenty-five years older than my mother, he looked and acted much younger. He actually lied about his real age until he was in his early nineties, when he proudly owned up to his longevity. My stepfather was solidly middle class, and my mother joined him in his export business as his secretary and bookkeeper. He was a very loving man. He legally adopted me and very soon I dropped the "step" in stepdaughter.

Along with a father, I also gained a sister. Zunia had a six-year-old daughter named Diana. She had been raised since infancy by a series of nannies in Manhattan. Before he married my mother, my overly generous father had surrounded himself with men of questionable influence—moochers who smoked, drank, and played cards. My mother knew this was no environment to raise a family, so we moved from Manhattan to Forest Hills, an upscale neighborhood near the famous tennis courts. Given her early upbringing, my sister, Diana, needed tender loving care, and my mother set out to provide just that.

Up until then, I was the center of my mother's universe. We had gone through so much together, and she treated me more like an equal than her child. I became very jealous of the attention my mother gave to Diana. I nursed my resentment while I attended Forest Hills High School, a suburban paradise with extensive sports fields and fairly good academics. I graduated in January 1954 with a medal in English and strong recommendations from my teachers to apply to college, but I decided instead to get married, partly because I wanted to leave behind my home situation that I still found so upsetting. I could not get over the feeling of having been marginalized in my family. I must insert here that as we grew older, despite the eight-year age difference, Diana and I became very close. My soon-to-be husband, Paul, and I helped see her through a divorce from her first husband, and the two of us lived through the loss of both our parents. She married a wonderful man, Shelly, who is a doctor, and they stood by me through my own losses and health challenges.

I had met my husband, Paul, when I was fourteen, during the summer my family rented a cottage in Long Beach. He was four years older and about to enter college in the fall. I fell madly in love as only a teenager can. In the context of today's sexual mores, the age difference may make it seem like a predatory relationship. But I was mature beyond my age and, given my strong sense of propriety, I was still a virgin on my wedding night.

We began a courtship that involved endless subway rides for him since I lived in Queens, and he lived in Brooklyn. Paul's parents introduced me to the Americanized side of the Jewish immigrant experience, having come to this country as toddlers at the beginning of the twentieth century. By the time

I met them in 1950, they were solid middle-class citizens, my father-in-law in a partnership with his brother in the watch business and my mother-in-law a stay-at-home wife and an excellent cook—I loved her gefilte fish and stuffed cabbage, two mainstays of Jewish cooking.

Because I had fallen in love, and because of my distress at having "lost" my mother, I determined that I would get married as soon as I graduated from high school, much to the dismay of my parents and my counselors. This was right in the middle of the Korean War. Paul missed passing the test that would have granted him a deferral to stay in college by just a few points. Unwilling to be drafted into the infantry, he enlisted in the air force in 1952 for a four-year stint. We continued our exclusive relationship, and I wrote him a letter every day from the time he left New York to do his basic training until we got married. I shared with Paul every detail of my life. I know it may seem quaint, but in the 1950s there were fewer societal distractions that today stand in the way of the kind of commitment Paul and I made to each other.

I graduated early from high school in January 1954 and did not intend to sit idle until our wedding, which was scheduled for September. In those days, for the most part, women had only two career options, to be a teacher or nurse. All my friends planned to become teachers. From my perspective, they were not wise enough to be entrusted with the development of children's minds. Of course, they were as immature as they had a right to be at their age, but I determined then and there that when I had children, they would go to private schools so that I could have some control over who would be teaching them.

We knew we would not get any kind of financial support from our parents, so even though I had only eight months before my wedding day, I took a job as a secretary at a sleazy firm in downtown Manhattan, where my boss literally chased me around the desk. Here I was, not even eighteen years old, completely inexperienced and coping with a very insistent older man who tried to convince me that I needed experience before I got married. He was claiming the *droit du seigneur* in twentieth-century America! Even though I was rather diffident in those days, I held him off. I can attest that the way *Mad Men,* the popular TV series (which was set in a much more sophisticated advertising agency in the 1960s), portrayed the treatment of women is entirely true to my experience in the 1950s.

Fast-forward decades later to when the MeToo movement brought to light the abominable behavior of men who use their power to subjugate and humiliate women. Despite laws meant to protect women and hold companies liable for tolerating abuse, women continue to be harassed in the workplace. It's not uncommon for perpetrators to have a complete lack of self-awareness: case in point, former New York governor Andrew Cuomo who, at the age of sixty-three, argued that it was a generational divide that led women in his orbit to misinterpret his behavior. Incredibly, former president Trump escaped any repercussions when, during his run for the presidency in 2016, it was reported that he had brazenly crowed in 2005 that if you are famous enough, women will let you grab them by their genitals. It amazes me that this sense of entitlement and predation still prevails.

As I was dealing with the unwanted advances of my boss, Paul was doing his basic training in upstate New York, a very trying experience for a sheltered young man who was something of a loner and did not respond well to authority. But in the days of the Korean War and conscription, there was no way to avoid the draft—back then no one would have even considered crossing the border to Canada to dodge the draft as many young men did during the Vietnam War. After a posting in Greenville, South Carolina, Paul was stationed in Saint John's, Newfoundland, at Pepperrell Air Force Base.

We saw each other only once during this time, midway through his posting, in 1953, when his parents, my parents, our respective sisters, and I met him on Prince Edward Island for a week. The next time we saw each other was when he was on leave for a week for our wedding. We got married on a beautiful day on September 26, 1954, at the Forest Hills Inn, a landmark in the upscale neighborhood where my parents had bought a modest house. We had an afternoon wedding, surrounded by family and friends. I still love looking at the iconic picture of Paul and I kissing at the end of the ceremony. It beautifully captures the culmination of our courtship. We honeymooned for three days at a charming inn in Croton-on-Hudson, a small, picturesque town in Westchester County just north of New York City. We then flew to where he was stationed at Pepperrell Air Force Base. The second time I ever flew was on a military plane with bucket seats and no amenities that was used to transport troops—a far cry from a commercial airline experience.

Off I went to start my life as an air force wife. Because he had the rank of sergeant, we did not qualify for on-base housing, which was reserved for higher-ranking enlisted men and officers. We rented two rooms in a small house—a bedroom and a combined kitchen, dining room, and living room that totaled about two hundred square feet, and we shared the bathroom with our landlords, who lived in the front three rooms. I worked as a secretary on the base, and Paul worked the job for which the air force had trained him, that of machine accountant.

There wasn't much to do in Saint John's, but we made friends with other young married couples and managed to have good times. We met people we never would have encountered in New York City, including our best friends, a couple from Moline, Illinois, whose names I have long since forgotten. The armed forces provided a melting pot experience at least as far as geography and lifestyles were concerned, but not so much when it came to race and ethnicity.

Because we shopped primarily at the commissary and were both very conservative with money, we accumulated considerable savings over the eighteen months we spent in Saint John's, which, added to the cash wedding presents we received (no wedding registry for us—that didn't exist in our milieu), added up to a $5,000 nest egg. Paul was discharged in April 1956, and we returned to New York in a late winter snowstorm. My parents picked us up at the airport with a welcome-home orchid corsage that looked quite out of place on the parka I wore.

Because I was just eighteen when I got married, I didn't have time to apply for citizenship and obtain it before I left. I entered Newfoundland on my valid French passport, and the first thing I did coming back to the United States was to apply for citizenship as the wife of an American citizen, which was a faster way of obtaining it. To become a citizen, you have to be eighteen years old and have been a permanent resident of the United States for five years, and I did not meet that criterion after living in Newfoundland for a year and a half.

As an immigrant who had suffered the extreme hardships of the Second World War, being sworn in was a very moving experience for me. My official entry into the American polity was a huge milestone, and I've taken the responsibilities of citizenship seriously since day one. I have voted in every single election since 1956, and my run for Congress in 1998 was the culmination of my desire to give back to the country that had given me so much.

When I look at the seemingly insoluble immigration

policy dilemma that America has grappled with for the last four decades, I wonder at the inability of Congress to come to a compromise. I wonder at it, but I understand it. Many Republicans fear that granting citizenship to illegal immigrants will result in an influx of voters more likely to vote Democratic. What I don't understand is why the Democrats, whose stated purpose is to help those who seek refuge in the United States, don't agree to do just that by granting them a permanent green card enabling them to enjoy the benefits that all resident aliens enjoy, but not the right to vote. After all, in entering the country illegally, they broke the law. Thereby their right to participate in voting is, in my view, disputable. However, as participants in the economy, it's undeniable that they deserve its benefits and the right to get out of the shadows that their status conveys.

CHAPTER 5

Flush with our savings after Paul's discharge, we bought a 1956 turquoise-and-white Chevrolet and went on a road trip. We stopped in Denver, a city we considered as a possible alternative to New York and where we were amazed to rub elbows with actual cowboys. We looped down to Florida, where I remember feeling very uncomfortable sitting in a bar as a couple of local yahoos talked about New York Jews in a derogatory fashion. The trip was an eye-opener for us. It revealed how immense America is and how diverse its population. It was like driving through different contiguous countries where everyone spoke English (but not with the same accent and cadence).

After our road trip, we decided to make New York City our home. We rented and furnished a modest one-bedroom apartment in Rego Park in Queens, and Paul went back to college to earn a degree in private accounting. In those days, student loans didn't exist, and middle-class parents did not subsidize the education of their adult children. As a veteran, Paul qualified for the GI Bill, the Servicemen's Readjustment Act of 1944, which provided a tuition stipend. It was a portal to upward mobility for many working-class veterans, and it unleashed the power of America's human capital, which led to the postwar prosperity the country enjoyed. This is yet another example of how the level of education of the population is a key determinant of a country's economic status.

Unfortunately, not all veterans had access to the benefits of the GI Bill. During the Jim Crow era, benefits to help veterans with education, housing, and unemployment insurance were deliberately withheld from Black veterans by legislators. It's outrageous and a disgrace that the country for which they fought denied Black men these benefits. To this day, that stain on America's history remains, despite the civil rights victories and increased opportunities available to the Black community. I do not take for granted that we were able to build a solid foundation because Paul benefited from the GI Bill, when many others did not have the same opportunity.

Both Paul and I found jobs in New York. Paul landed a job at IBM thanks to the training he had gotten in the air force. I took a position as a secretary in the French American export firm that had employed my mother before she remarried. A year after our return, we moved to Manhattan, that mecca of young, ambitious people. By then, chafing at having to wear a hat and not happy about the rigidity of Big Blue's corporate structure, which was reminiscent of what he thoroughly disliked about the air force, Paul left IBM to pursue an opportunity that today we'd call a start-up.

In the 1950s, companies were becoming more interested in using computers for payroll, accounts receivable, and other business functions. But the computers of the 1950s were enormous in size and prohibitively expensive. Companies couldn't afford to purchase and house these behemoths. That led to the rise of service bureaus, companies that leased computers, installed them in large climate-controlled spaces, and ran applications for their business clients. At the time, computers ran on punch cards, but Paul's knowledge of these primitive models gave him a leading edge in the burgeoning tech industry. The two founding partners of a firm called Statistics for Management approached Paul. The partners were visionaries and salesmen, but they needed someone to run operations. That's where Paul's training in the air force paid off. He became a junior partner without having to make a monetary investment.

Things were looking up for us. In the summer of 1958, we took a trip to France, the first time I had returned to my birthplace. There, I reconnected with my childhood friend Dora, who lived in the same building I did in Paris before the war, and with whom I had gone to school. She and her family had survived the war, and she married Jean-Claude Peretz, a photographer whose mother had been killed in the Holocaust. They had a Citroën Deux Chevaux, a tin-can car, in which we zipped through Paris. It was bittersweet to visit the land of my birth. Everything seemed so much smaller than I remembered—especially when compared to the larger-than-life environment of New York City. Of course, the streets of Paris brought back difficult memories of the war, but also it was a thrill to share with Paul the beauty of French culture and the delights of its culinary offerings.

But our trip held a surprise for us. At the Eiffel Tower, after unceremoniously upchucking, I realized that I was pregnant. Even though we had been married for more than three years, this was an unplanned pregnancy. Upon our return, we had to rethink our living arrangements. We couldn't bring a baby into our small Manhattan apartment, so we moved back to Queens, into a larger apartment across the street from my parents. I continued to work until the very last day of my pregnancy, my water breaking during the night ten days before my due date.

CHAPTER 6

Michèle was born in 1958, when I was twenty-two years old. We named her after my late maternal grandmother, Mira. It is the Jewish custom to name children with the first letter of a close relative who passed away. The pregnancy was uneventful, but Michèle had a very unusual birth. We didn't know it at the time, but Paul and I had an intragroup incompatibility. We were both positive, his blood type being A and mine being O, but while Michèle was in the birth canal, my body identified her as a threat and sent antibodies to eliminate it. At first, we didn't suspect anything was wrong. When she was a few hours old and I held her in my arms for the first time, her skin had such a tawny hue that I told her she looked like she had just come back from Florida with a tan. In the middle of the night, a cluster of doctors woke me to tell me that she had jaundice and that they needed to do a complete blood transfusion, reopening her navel and replacing her compromised blood supply with blood compatible with Paul's blood type. My obstetrician knew of intragroup incompatibility but had never encountered the condition in his thirty years of practice.

I will forever be grateful to the intern who spotted Michèle's jaundice. She was actually a fully licensed doctor in her native country, but she had to redo her medical training when she immigrated to the United States. She saved my daughter's life.

In the 1950s, when middle-class women had children, they stopped working. This was true of every single one of our friends. But I knew myself and I knew that staying home would be so detrimental to my mental health. Paul supported my decision to go back to work, which was highly unusual in our milieu. We hired a nanny and, six weeks after Michèle was born, I returned to my desk. Mind you, I did not have a glamorous or lucrative career; I was a secretary who took dictation and typed. Still, I knew that being a stay-at-home mom was not for me. I worried about the boredom, and earning a salary helped us to achieve the lifestyle we aspired to. We hired full-time, live-in nannies including, as the children got older, a series of au pairs from Iceland, who stayed one year and then arranged for their replacement to take over when they moved on. We and several other families used this Icelandic pipeline for years.

In the meantime, Paul's company flourished, and we moved back to Manhattan into a large but very old-fashioned Upper East Side apartment. In the summers we spent our weekends renting modest cottages in East Hampton, an upscale beach community on Long Island. There we met an entirely different group of people including our best friends, Lois and Danny Bloom, two very sophisticated New Yorkers with exceptional social graces. Paul and I loved fine food and could hold our own when it came to appraising wines, but through Lois and Danny we learned to appreciate opera and to partake in a much more cultured life in Manhattan than the life we left behind in Queens. In 1972, the four of us took a memorable driving trip through France and toured all the Michelin three-star restaurants. On one of our forays in Alsace, we inadvertently came up to a toll crossing on the border of Germany. I prevailed upon the border official to allow us to make an illegal U-turn. I had determined never to step foot in that country, and I never have.

Next to family, I've learned that friendship is the most essential component of a good life. As Aristotle writes in the *Nicomachean Ethics*, "For without friends, no one would choose to live, though he had all other goods." My friendship with Lois and Danny lasted more than sixty years. They moved from New York to Saint Helena, a lovely California town in the Napa Valley and a short car ride from where we eventually settled in San Francisco. I considered their home my country retreat and often spent my weekends there. Paul and I always worried about Danny's longevity. He was an excellent cook, loved butter, never exercised, and his father died of a heart attack at the age of forty-five. We needn't have worried, though. Danny lived to celebrate his ninety-third birthday and passed away in September 2021. Lois passed away from COVID-19 at the age of ninety in 2020. As you age and lose one friend after the other, you learn to come to terms with your own mortality, and you realize that fewer and fewer people in the world know you.

We are social animals and much of the happiness we enjoy comes from sharing our lives with others. Another friend I'm grateful to have shared decades with is Naomi Siegmann. We knew each other for almost sixty-two years. I met Naomi when we returned to New York in 1956 (she was the token American in the French firm for which I worked). She and her husband, Henry, moved to Mexico City in 1959, but we kept in close contact and spent a great deal of time together in Mexico and overseas. On one such adventure we took a cruise around the Greek Islands. The Aegean is very turbulent, and midcruise, while taking a shower in our cabin, I slipped in the bathtub and could not get up. I had injured my right arm, but there was nothing to be done until we returned to land. In Athens I learned I had broken my ulna. I was put in a temporary cast, and once back in New York, I had to have two separate surgeries to ensure the bone set properly. The five-inch scar remains on my left arm, commemorating that trip and reminding me of my dear friends and the time we shared together.

Henry died in 1986 from leukemia at the age of fifty-eight. Although Naomi remained in Mexico, we managed to maintain our close relationship. We regularly talked and continued to share the joys and sorrows of our lives. We traveled together and confided in one another about the successes and challenges our children faced. We spent three exciting weeks in Japan following an itinerary arranged by a travel agent because it would have been hard to navigate in that country where little English is spoken, and the culture is very different. Naomi died at the age of eighty-four in March 2018.

I truly believe that the success we achieve at any level is dependent on our interactions with others. The friendships I have made, both personal and professional, have held me in good stead. These friends have sustained me through some of my darkest moments; they've shared in my triumphs; and they have brought me immeasurable joy.

When my son Gerald was born five and a half years after the birth of Michèle, the probability of him developing intragroup incompatibility was exceptionally high, so the doctor left his umbilical cord untied, measuring his bilirubin over a period of a few hours. Ultimately, he required a blood transfusion, but this time, the hospital was prepared. We named Gerald after my late father, Grisha, or Gregoire in French.

It was a time of great social unrest in the United States. I was four months pregnant with Gerald when President

Kennedy was assassinated. Most of us who were alive at the time remember exactly where we were when we heard the news. Paul and I had met his sister for lunch at a diner on the East Side when the news came over the radio. It was a devastating event, and we were all glued to our televisions, watching in real time as Jack Ruby shot and killed Lee Harvey Oswald, President Kennedy's assassin. In sorrow, we watched the funeral procession and the unforgettable image of the president's son, then three-year-old John-John, saluting as it went by.

President Kennedy's assassination not only represented the loss of a great man but also the loss of innocence for America. The charismatic, handsome president, his glamorous wife, and their young family epitomized hope. His death coincided with the stirrings of the civil rights movement that Martin Luther King Jr. and his followers had set in motion some ten years earlier. The movement gained wide national attention with the march on Washington, DC, in 1963, when Dr. King made his famous "I Have a Dream" speech three months before President Kennedy was shot. Many phrases in that speech deeply resonated with Americans and are still cited today. The phrase that I find most persuasive is "I have a dream that one day this nation will rise up and live out the true meaning of its creed: 'We hold these truths to be self-evident: that all men are created equal.'"

The civil rights movement challenged the untenable doctrines of Jim Crow, and it also gave birth to the women's liberation movement and the gay rights movement. The year 1963 was a turning point for this country. If a single individual could assassinate a country's chosen leader, then nothing was sacrosanct—no institution, no tradition, no custom. More and more people began to question the status quo.

With the advent of televised news, the momentous events

of that period reached the living rooms of most of the population. Witnessing events firsthand changed America forever. We saw Jack Ruby shoot Lee Harvey Oswald in real time; we saw law enforcement officers train water hoses on the marchers in Selma, Alabama; night after night we saw the tragic footage of the body bags in Vietnam; we saw the protesters at the Chicago Democratic Convention in 1968 attacked by the police; we saw four students shot and killed by the National Guard in a protest at Kent State in Ohio.

Witnessing these events led to a cultural revolution not only in the United States but all over the world. People saw with their own eyes the types of tragedies that previously were filtered through radio or newspapers. When you see how the sausage is made, you begin to question the cook. And if the cook refuses to answer, you take matters into your own hands. It is hard for those born after 1965 to understand what an incredible shift occurred between the launch of the TV series *Leave It to Beaver* in October 1957 and the explosive televised events of the '60s that led a new generation to seek answers outside of the establishment and to embrace a new mindset. Across the world we heard liberating mantras such as "let it all hang out," "do your own thing," and "never trust anyone over thirty."

These were heady times for people of my generation. We had lived through the Second World War and been brought up in a straitlaced manner in the years after. Even the music of the time was liberating. The beat was intoxicating. We reveled in the sounds of the Rolling Stones, the Beatles, and the Grateful Dead. We danced the twist, the hully-gully, and the watusi, and we danced alone or in groups—a big departure from the staid choreographed dances of the past.

Among my memorabilia from that period, I have a picture that was published in *Life* magazine in the '60s of me dancing in a crowd at a hot spot in East Hampton. I'm wearing a fall, which is a wig of long hair, with flipped ends à la Jacqueline Kennedy; a tunic; and wide-legged pants in a voile summer print. I love to dance, and I remember how exhilarating it was for me to move to the driving beats with no inhibition. This type of dancing is commonplace these days, but back then it felt revolutionary. It was a radical departure from the past.

Another extreme divergence from earlier times was the widespread casual use of drugs, mostly marijuana. My circle of friends smoked pot recreationally, on weekends. For me, it heightened the feeling of freedom and of living life at a more intense level. In those days, marijuana, or what we called "Mary Jane," was not as powerful as it is today. However, I recall one experience that made me realize the potential danger of the drug. Paul and I and Lois and Danny were vacationing in Barbados, staying at the same hotel as a well-known British movie star and his entourage. As we sat together on the lawn after dinner, they offered us some tokes. After a few puffs, my buzz felt entirely different from usual. I became aware that the Brits were baiting Danny in a verbally threatening manner. My survival instincts kicked in, and I remember using a nonsensical phrase about not liking this channel and having to change it. I got out of my chair with great effort and insisted that we all needed to go back to our room to watch the channel we wanted. It turned out that the marijuana was laced with something that made it much more powerful. That was a lesson learned: don't smoke with people you don't know, and don't use pot of unknown provenance.

I don't want to give you the idea that we were druggies. Far from it. We continued to work hard at our respective jobs and raise the children. In 1967, Paul's company went public and did quite well in the initial offering. After he sold some of his stock, we came into $450,000 (the equivalent of about

$3 million today), quite a windfall for us. We bought a charming second home on a cul-de-sac in Ridgefield, Connecticut, and put in a pool on our three-and-a-half-acre plot. Several luminaries lived in the area. One of our neighbors was Alvin Toffler, author of the international bestseller *Future Shock*. He foresaw the challenges of how the increasing rate of change in the world would affect individuals and society. We had dinner with him once and were fascinated by this visionary. Given the state of the world today, I marvel at how prescient he was.

During that period, American Express acquired Paul's company and he had to adjust to a new, very rigid corporate culture. His job became very demanding, and he had to be available around the clock. By the end of 1969, at the age of thirty-seven, he left the company and retired. He never held a full-time job again.

During this time, I, too, decided to quit my job. I still didn't have the temperament to be a full-time mom, so I took an inconsequential part-time job for a short while. However, that didn't satisfy my need for a challenge. Because I didn't need to bring in a salary, in 1968, I enrolled as a full-time student at Hunter College, located at walking distance from our apartment on the East Side of Manhattan. At the age of thirty-two, I picked up where I left off after high school and finally found where I belonged.

When I look back on my educational experience in America, I am amazed how much I changed from the time I attended PS 2 in the South Bronx to the time I graduated with a PhD from Columbia University. I was always a very good student because I applied myself and I was very well organized, but I had no intellectual curiosity, and my writing was pedestrian. The medal I earned in English was not a recognition for my creative writing ability, but rather for my grasp of grammar and the clarity of my arguments. I can't remember ever reading a nonfiction book that was not part of an assignment. I always enjoyed reading, but mostly I read mysteries and action books. I'm glad that I postponed going to college, because when I finally applied at the age of thirty-two, I was prepared to take full advantage of the intellectual journey.

CHAPTER 7

Hunter College is a public institution, and in 1968, tuition was $55 per semester. Because I loved New York City, I contemplated majoring in urban planning, a new discipline focused on making cities more livable at all levels. It became quickly apparent to me that to be an effective urban planner, I'd have to develop an understanding of politics. I decided to major in political science and, again, I found that to understand that discipline, I needed to understand the fundamental ideas that informed political philosophy. I eagerly read all the great books, pre-Socratic to post-Marxist. In 1970, a cultural revolution was sweeping through the western world as the anti–Vietnam War movement was sweeping through the nation's colleges. Meanwhile, Hunter College was in the throes of a governance struggle that pitted entrenched and obstinate faculty members against students agitating for a voice in the school administration, which historically had been the exclusive privilege of the faculty council. At that time, in an attempt to open the doors to underserved and underrepresented students, the City University of New York had implemented the newly established open admissions policy, which abandoned objective standards of college readiness and allowed any high school graduate to enroll. This resulted in an influx of minority students who wanted their educational experience to reflect their reality.

Because of the unrest, Hunter College closed in late April and didn't formally reopen for the rest of the semester. Rather than attending class, we attended consciousness-raising sessions. One such session was led by a charismatic Marxist professor. He invited a Black African to share with us the anguish of worshipping a white god. The speaker went on and on about the experience, always using the pronoun "he" to describe the deity. Finally, I called out, "You mean 'she,' don't you?" This tendency to speak out when the spirit moves me was not unusual for me at that time. Although I was rather shy and diffident as a child and always well behaved, as I grew older, I gained confidence and I became considerably bolder. When I taught a course pro bono at Dominican College in San Rafael, California, in 1993, I warned the students on the first day of the semester, "This is a course entirely about dead, white European males. If this offends your sensibilities in any way, you should probably withdraw now." Not surprisingly, up until the twentieth century, there were no women of any consequence in the pantheon of political philosophers—not only in the Western tradition but in other traditions as well. I was never politically correct even before that term gained the currency it enjoys now.

As weeks went by with the school still closed, I became more and more willing to assert my beliefs. In a session about police brutality and unlawful shootings in the Black community, the discussion focused on the oppression Black people experienced and the fear they lived under. To me, nothing compared to the murder of six million Jews and seven million others (Catholic priests, Communists, homosexuals, Romani, and mentally challenged people), a total of thirteen million people murdered by the Nazis *because of who they were.* And I said so because for me, America represented the best system of government ever created for a heterogeneous society living under the rule of law. Our system is not ideal by any means, but as James Madison wrote in *The Federalist Papers,* "If men were angels, no government would be necessary. If angels were to govern men, neither external nor internal controls on government would be necessary."

I have outgrown that point of view. In retrospect, I have come to understand that people suffer in many different ways under many different circumstances, and none are comparable, nor can they be rated on any scale. Life is an untenable nightmare if you constantly fear for your safety. I'm reminded of an anecdote that Isabel Wilkinson cites in her book *Caste: The Origins of our Discontents* about a student essay contest that took place in 1944 in Columbus, Ohio. The topic was what should be done with Adolf Hitler after the war ended. A sixteen-year-old Black girl won the contest with this answer: "Put him in a black skin and let him live the rest of his life in America."

During the students' strike at Hunter College, a group of Black activists rose in prominence on campus. They echoed the ideology of the Black Panther Party, which originated in Oakland, California, in 1966. Their rallying cry was "All Power to the People," a mantra that had arisen out of the many revolutionary movements of the period. During an assembly in the overflowing Hunter College auditorium, the leaders of this group harangued the crowd about continuing to keep the school shut down. It was more than I could take. I got up on the stage, claimed, "I'm a people, too," and expressed the silent majority's sentiments that classes should resume. Most of the students were first-generation college students seizing the opportunity made possible by the newly implemented New York City open admissions policy. These students were not part of the very vocal minority of insurgents whose aim was to further their agenda and assert their power, and I firmly believed that their point of view needed to be shared.

Even though I opposed the Vietnam War and supported equal rights, I was considered conservative because I wanted classes to resume. I did not think it was fair that I be deprived of my opportunity for education, nor did I think that other students, most of them women from lower-income homes, should be deprived, either. Hunter College at the Lexington Avenue campus had become co-ed in 1964 and was predominantly female. Many of the women in my classes were the first in their families to attend college and had to fight for the opportunity. They had to overcome the prejudice against educating women, because at the time many still viewed higher education for women as worthless.

Regarding the Vietnam War, however, I was determinedly against it. At one point, I spoke at a rally near Wall Street, standing in front of several hundred people and emphatically saying, "I have a six-year-old son and he's not going!" This was the second war America did not win—the first being the Korean War, which had changed the course of Paul's life and mine. Do you know that there are still 28,500 members of the American armed forces stationed in South Korea? And since the end of that war, North Korea has become a rogue state that has nuclear bombs. As for the Vietnam War, who can forget our ignominious departure from that country in April 1975?

Unfortunately, we did not learn our lessons from Vietnam, as evidenced by our twenty years in Afghanistan, the longest-lasting undeclared war in American history, where we conveniently forgot the truism that Afghanistan is the graveyard of empires. Britain fought there not once, not twice, but three times, the last being in 1919. Then the Russians had their turn, spending ten years there before leaving in defeat in 1989. War has become a business under the control of hawks who are in the thrall of arms merchants. When President Eisenhower cautioned us to beware of the military-industrial complex in his farewell speech in 1961, he could never have imagined that the Afghanistan War would cost the US taxpayers $300 million a day for twenty years. In the meantime, we can't afford to alleviate the suffering of the 40 percent of Americans who don't have $400 in the bank to meet an unexpected expense. As I write this, we've just made a disastrous exit from Afghanistan. Although the administration did manage to extract more than one hundred thousand people in a daredevil evacuation, only time will tell what sort of repercussions we'll see from our ill-advised war in Afghanistan.

Because I was outspoken and older than the majority of my fellow students, the faculty selected me to represent the students on Hunter College's Faculty Committee of the Political Science Department. While I was honored to be chosen, that experience gave me an unwelcome glimpse of the petty politics of academia. I witnessed so much struggle among the council's members for very little power. It was amazing to watch the battles of the egos. I saw full tenured professors being prima donnas and bringing little of worth to the classroom, lecturing from notes yellowed with age, rehashing lessons they'd written decades before.

Despite the social unrest on campus, I loved my college experience. You know the old saying, "youth is wasted on the young," but equally true is that education is wasted on the young. Going straight from high school to college isn't always the best option for a young mind. When only elites had access to higher education, its function was clearly defined—to train leaders for the ruling class. But when it became democratized, it morphed into extended career training. You went to college either to get a good job or because you didn't quite know what else to do. When my son, Gerald, attended Harvard, Paul and I had a serious discussion with him about his major, the history of science. Paul wanted to know where that would lead in terms of a career and how he saw his life moving forward, and Gerald replied, "Dad, Harvard is not a trade school." As a freshman in January 1982, Gerald wrote us a letter musing on this subject, in which he says, in part, "I have known that I am special in some way, and being at Harvard has only reaffirmed that knowledge. This realization is dangerous because I feel as if I will be of major importance in my lifetime to the whole world." This from a young man who had not yet turned eighteen.

CHAPTER 8

After Paul left American Express in 1969, we found ourselves in a peculiar situation in our social milieu in Manhattan. Most of our friends were much better off than we were and had upper-middle-class origins, as opposed to our solidly lower-middle-class roots. Truth be told, neither one of us were big spenders. Because we were fiscally prudent, even with neither one of us earning a salary, we managed to live at a good Upper East Side address and send our children to prestigious private schools (Michèle at the Brearley School and Gerald at the Trinity School). We had a second home in the country and took trips abroad. We liked convertibles, so our cars were first a midline Chrysler and then a midline Buick, but I had no jewelry to speak of, no furs, and we always looked for bargains. Paul didn't believe in buying on credit and we never lived beyond our means. We did love to travel and in 1970, we toured Europe with our children for five weeks. We also traveled several times without them. In our generation, children were an appendage; family life centered entirely on the adults. It would never have entered our minds to make dinner reservations at a

Manhattan restaurant with friends and to bring our children along.

The milieu in which we moved was extremely competitive. As soon as you joined a group of people in a social setting, the conversation always started with "What do you do?" or "Where do you live?" and "Where do your children go to school?" If you passed muster, the conversation might continue until your interlocutor saw someone more important enter the room. For Paul and me, the first question was the killer. Here he was, a young man who didn't work. Here I was, a full-time student. While our longtime friends embraced our choices, it was difficult for those new to us to understand why we weren't as fiscally ambitious as most people at that time.

I was totally immersed in my college experience, but Paul had to find ways to fill his time. Although he had always been interested in politics and the arts, he hadn't pursued those subjects at college, so he enrolled at the New School, a well-known, progressive university in Greenwich Village that offered continuing education. Luckily, given both our schedules, we were able to spend quite a bit of time at our house in Ridgefield, Connecticut, with our children and our newly acquired pet, a Siberian husky we named Nicholas. We enjoyed the peaceful and rural setting, where we could indulge in our passion for reading—his as an autodidact and mine in the service of studying for the courses I was taking.

I graduated summa cum laude from Hunter College in 1973 and was accepted to the Graduate School of Arts and Sciences at Columbia University and started there that fall. I received a merit scholarship that paid my tuition for the first year. I majored in political science with an emphasis on political philosophy. The more I delved into the eternal questions that underlie human nature and the social order, the more interested I became in exploring the answers. And I still am to this day, as you will see when you read the rest of my musings. My dissertation sponsor was Professor Herbert Deane. As an administrator of the university in 1968, he dismissed student opinions on the administration without reasoned explanations as having no more importance than if the student had said they liked the taste of strawberries. This became known as the "Strawberry Statement" around campus and reflected the chasm between the establishment and the surge of youth challenging authority.

Professor Deane was a courtly gentleman in the full meaning of that word—a gentle man. He was caught up in the vortex of a revolution that brought into question not only the trappings of authority but the validity of what it espoused. I remember a conversation we had (we were more kindred spirits than not—after all, I had voted for Goldwater in 1964) in which he decried the fact that he could no longer assume that students in his graduate classes had any knowledge of the Bible. To explain the basis for the rule of one man over others, and man's willingness to accept that rule, which harks back to the covenant between the people of Israel and their first king, Saul, he had to teach that part of the Bible first. This was a big change for a man who had started teaching at Columbia in 1948.

I had a very difficult time choosing a topic for my dissertation. I loved the Greek philosophers, but Professor Deane insisted that to tackle them, I needed to learn ancient Greek to meet the rigorous standards of the department. There was no way, he argued, that I could do original work on Plato if I couldn't read Plato in the original. Ultimately, I decided to go the modern route and write about a contemporary philosopher, John Rawls. I critiqued his book *A Theory of Justice*, originally published in 1971 and revised in 1975. His was a modern revival of the social contract theory, which I am not going to discuss any further for fear of losing you, dear reader.

Writing a dissertation is trial by fire, especially in my case because I was typing it myself on an electric typewriter with no self-correcting mechanism. Imagine meeting the stylistic requirements of a scholarly document that runs over three hundred pages without the miraculous features of cut-and-paste, page previews, and footnote templates. I started in 1976 just as we were seriously contemplating a move to the West Coast. My sister had moved to Silicon Valley and my sister-in-law had moved to Los Angeles. When our parents retired, rather than move to Florida as is often the case with Jewish retirees who want to escape the brutal New York winters, they moved to California, where their daughters already resided.

Because we were somewhat adrift in New York and because the pull of family was very strong, Paul and I decided to move to San Francisco. Although a much smaller city than New York, it was the only city cosmopolitan enough for us to consider as a home. It has world-class opera, the symphony, ballet companies, and even more important for foodies like us, it boasts a plethora of terrific restaurants. In the summer of 1977, we found a charming flat in Pacific Heights, an upscale San Francisco neighborhood. Unfortunately, no pets were allowed, so we had to give Nicholas back to the breeder—which was traumatic for all of us.

Gerald would attend San Francisco University High School, an excellent private high school conveniently located two doors down from our flat. Michèle had moved to Colorado Springs to attend Colorado College. She had been an indifferent student at the Brearley School, struggling to juggle several subjects at a time. Colorado College complemented her learning style with its block system, where she took courses one at a time over a period of three and a half weeks. Concentrating on one topic at a time dramatically changed her academic performance. She went from a C+ student in high school to the dean's list every year at Colorado College. Unfortunately, at that time resources didn't exist to help us discover earlier that Michèle was best suited for the block system or to find a school that offered it. It is only in recent years that we're understanding the importance of how children learn, and I'll have more to say about this in later chapters.

CHAPTER 9

We moved to San Francisco on July 7, 1977 (7/7/77), hiring a couple of college students to drive our Buick convertible across the country. As soon as we arrived, I offered my services as a volunteer at Gerald's school, hoping to meet people in our new city. San Francisco University High School was only four years old at the time, led by a very charismatic headmaster, Dennis Collins. As it happened, the school was just embarking on a fundraising event to generate scholarship opportunities for lower-income students. The event was the San Francisco Decorator Showcase, in which the school obtained the use of a mansion for six months, during which time a group of designers selected by the design committee refurbished it, and the school opened it to the public for three weeks. It was a very complicated, labor-intensive endeavor, and when I arrived just two months before the opening, I was warmly welcomed as a volunteer. The committee soon found that I happen to be very efficient and conscientious.

While volunteering that first year, we met two couples

who would turn out to be our very best friends in our new home. Like us, Jean and Jim Douglas had recently moved to San Francisco. They were from Michigan and their life experience could not have been more different from ours. Jim was a very successful businessman, and they had commissioned the world-renowned architect Richard Meier to build a home for them on a spectacular lot in Harbor Springs, overlooking Lake Michigan. The home was known as the Douglas House.

We also befriended longtime San Francisco residents Birgit and Michael Hall. They were big-city people but, like Jean and Jim, they were non-Jews with none of the reference points that make New York Jews a tribe unto itself. In fact, this was the first time that we had gentile friends. Happily, that did not stand in the way of establishing very strong relationships. Both families had a son at University High School, and we were all very involved in the showcase. Birgit and I took on the job of chair and co-chair of the next showcase. The 1977 showcase netted $6,000 for the scholarship fund. Since then and until 2019 (the last year the showcase was held before the pandemic), the event has raised a total of $16 million for the scholarship program.

Putting on the event was very complex. The first step was to find a home to take over for six months. After the house was obtained, the designers were invited for a day to view the rooms and to submit proposals. A design committee, which over the years always included one or two master designers, then selected the participants, making sure that the individual designs flowed smoothly from one room to the next. Only established designers could afford to decorate the larger rooms like the living, dining, and master bedrooms. But younger, less well-known ones often started with a second bedroom or a library or even a closet (famously, in 1979, we had a "primal scream closet," a tiny space where you could retire to deal with your demons) and graduated to the major rooms as their reputations grew along with their revenues.

Because of my early involvement, in 1980 Dennis Collins hired me as the school's first director of development. I was in charge of raising funds above and beyond the tuition revenue. Tuition never covers the full cost of running a private school. For a school to stay competitive, the tuition must remain as low as possible. It's expected that those parents who can will contribute generously to capital campaigns and annual fund drives. The school then supplements with fundraisers such as the Decorator Showcase, which puts the school in an excellent financial position.

This job opportunity was a real departure for me, but other than a part-time job teaching political philosophy at Golden Gate University in downtown San Francisco, I hadn't found a permanent academic position. I was eager to expand my horizons and confident enough in my organizational and administrative skills to take on the job. Paul found a niche for himself—using his training as a private accountant—working for H&R Block, helping people with their returns during tax season. The rest of the year he thoroughly explored the city and read voraciously, immersing himself in many of the books on my graduate school reading list.

Because I had no prior fundraising experience, Dennis sent me to a one-week summer training session put on by the National Association of Independent Schools (NAIS) at a college in New Hampshire, where I learned the basics of fundraising in a private school setting. I had never been to such an event and thoroughly enjoyed it. It brought together people from all over the country, giving me an opportunity to appreciate how diverse the field was. I would subsequently become NAIS's representative at the annual large conferences put on by the West Coast colleges and universities that included an independent school track. That experience held me in good stead for the next step in my career.

In addition, Dennis agreed to allow me to teach an elective political philosophy course in the History Department—so I was both an administrator and an instructor. I had no idea how difficult it would be to teach high schoolers—even in the best of circumstances with a group of well-behaved, well-educated students. It was a major challenge to impart my knowledge to young people whose reference points were a generation removed from mine. Lessons that touched on World War II, the Cold War, cultural revolution, or the civil rights struggle did not resonate with them. In retrospect, I was not a good teacher, because I was more inclined to pontificate and really didn't know how to engage my students in discussions. I do think that exposing them to the materials was a valuable experience, but my stint in that profession makes me reject the old trope "Those who can, do; those who can't, teach."

I became the director of development in 1980, and over the twelve years of my tenure, I had the opportunity to meet and work with well-established community members such as Ray Dolby, Mimi Haas of the Levi Strauss family, and the San Francisco socialite and philanthropist Dede Wilsey, among others. I worked closely with the chair of the development committee, Jerry Hume, who would become the first contributor to my congressional run and later my employer. I also worked closely with my dear friend Bill Oberndorf, who played a big role in my life, as you will hear in later chapters.

Through my position as director of development, Paul and I made many friends over the years. Unlike New York, you don't have to run the gauntlet with San Franciscans. If you are where they are, they assume you belong, and they don't give you the third degree to determine your place in society. We had wonderful times with our new friends, exploring the West Coast and taking full advantage of the culinary delights of San Francisco. Although we had traveled abroad several times, we found fewer reasons to take vacations in faraway places, the Bay Area being a bit of heaven on earth.

CHAPTER 10

We loved San Francisco and decided to settle into a neighborhood at the edge of Sea Cliff. As we prepared for our move from the flat we had rented on Jackson Street, I came across a note in Michèle's room that, at the time, sent me reeling. On a piece of paper, she'd written her signature with her college friend's last name appended to her own, much like a teenager in love will practice her married name. My heart stopped because her friend was a woman. We immediately called her at Colorado College, and she confirmed that she was a lesbian.

Michèle had always been a tomboy, but Paul and I considered it a phase. I routinely bought her feminine clothes, which she shunned as she got older. I remember that when she was fifteen, I realized that she had a crush on a summer camp counselor, and I had a talk with her about what that might lead to. She didn't date, but many of her high school friends also just hung out together, so we chalked it up to the fact that she attended an all-girls school. As a college freshman, she brought home a rich Texan man she had met at school, who was obviously taken with her. It didn't last long, although it did temporarily reassure us.

Remember that in 1979, the gay community was still very much in the closet. Strangely, the first thing I did when I saw that piece of paper was worry about how I would deal with it vis-à-vis my family and my friends. I worried about how I would manage the predictable questions about her meeting someone, about arranging for her to get together with this one's nephew or that one's brother, and about her getting married. My immediate instinct, which I followed for the next several years, was to keep it a secret.

I was distraught not only because of how I thought it would affect me, but also because of the stigma and challenges I feared she would face. Michèle recently told me that before she came out to us, she thought that I would be the understanding parent and that Paul would go ballistic. In fact, it was just the reverse and it shocked her.

I couldn't face the thought that my daughter would never have children and would never have what I considered a normal life. In other words, I couldn't face the thought that she would never follow the path I followed. At first, I was convinced that she could overcome this, that she could change her tendency, that it was more a matter of lifestyle than something ordained at birth. At my insistence, Paul and I spent many hours trying to persuade her, offering to send her to a therapist, threatening to disown her. We demanded that she come out to her grandparents, hoping that would make her change her ways. When she did come out to them, they were bewildered and concerned. I know it may be hard for you to understand how difficult this situation was for me. Looking back, it is hard for me to understand as well, but it's very challenging to overcome societal paradigms, and those were different times with different mores.

Gradually, the family adjusted to the situation. Michèle graduated from college and went to law school at Arizona State University in Tempe, and Gerald graduated from high school and went off to Harvard University. Our parents were growing old gracefully and we saw them frequently. Our move to the West Coast was proving to be the right choice on many different fronts.

We continued to enjoy a rich social life, but in the early eighties the AIDS epidemic started to decimate the gay community. This dreadful disease affected many of the designer friends we had met through the Decorator Showcase, and we were directly touched by the increasing number of deaths in that community. It was heartbreaking to witness the deaths of so many talented young men felled by a disease for which there was no cure. The handling of the epidemic by the Reagan administration reflected the attitudes toward gay people at the time: fear, condemnation, and neglect. AIDS sufferers were shunned. People panicked about exposure even though it was clear that the disease was contracted only through the exchange of bodily fluids. Many saw the disease as the wrath of God brought down on promiscuous sinners. Having a gay daughter made me even more compassionate to the plight of the gay community during the height of the AIDS epidemic. It's an immense relief that scientists have discovered drugs to stave off HIV-related deaths through lifelong drug treatments. It was Dr. Anthony Fauci, the current hero of the COVID-19 pandemic, who helped orchestrate this groundbreaking protocol.

In the summer of 1985, our daughter became a lawyer and went to work at Brown & Bain, a Silicon Valley law firm that brought her back home. Michèle had two partners while she worked in Silicon Valley. The first relationship was short-lived and the second resulted in a commitment ceremony officiated by a nondenominational minister, because gay marriage was not legal at that time. My mother, my visiting aunt, and I attended in the backyard of the house that Michèle shared with her partner and her two children. Eventually, the relationship ended. Michèle sold her house, became interested in writing, and moved to Taos, New Mexico, where she met a wonderful, talented woman, Natalie Goldberg, the author of *Writing Down the Bones*—the how-to manual for putative writers that has become a classic—and many other books.

CHAPTER 11

When Paul and I traveled to Boston to see Gerald graduate, Paul was feeling out of sorts, and over the next few months, he began to lose weight. Nothing dramatic, but with increasing pain in his lower back, he checked in with our family doctor, an excellent diagnostician. In May 1986, the doctor saw a shadow in Paul's X-rays and scheduled an exploratory operation for June 2. We were concerned, and my parents insisted they stay with me while Paul was in surgery. At the time, my father was ninety-four years old but as spry as ever. They were with me when the surgeon came into the waiting room and told us that Paul had terminal pancreatic cancer. The surgeon had performed a bypass operation on his digestive system to make whatever time he had left as comfortable as possible.

I will never forget that moment. I was overcome with grief and panicked about how to handle the situation. Paul had always been the dominant person in our relationship. We had been married thirty-two years and had an established rhythm that kept our marriage on an even keel. I didn't know what I'd do without him. I didn't know how I'd handle losing someone

I loved so much, whose life had been my life for so many years. But I couldn't give in to my panic. I couldn't let him down. I decided that I would filter all of my actions through the prism of this determination: after Paul dies, I will not regret doing this. That determination kept me strong through the thirteen months that Paul survived, and I shared my mantra with my friends who were living through similar circumstances with their partners during the AIDS epidemic.

Paul had a strained relationship with his hardheaded father, and when he learned of his prognosis, he insisted that we keep it a secret from his parents. Ever since they moved to Los Angeles in 1976, I called them every Sunday and Paul occasionally got on the phone. As he became sicker, I continued to call them on schedule, making up excuses for why he couldn't come to the phone. His sister, Gloria, who was four years younger than me and with whom I had a very close relationship, knew, and had to abide by Paul's wishes as well. It wasn't until the very end that I told his parents he was in the hospital. Gloria notified them in person when he died. As you can imagine, keeping Paul's illness a secret from his parents added another layer of stress for me, but I could not overrule Paul's wish. My mother-in-law Anne died a year later, shortly thereafter followed by my father-in-law, Lou.

A few weeks after Paul's diagnosis, I was due to celebrate my fiftieth birthday. The plans for a birthday dinner for family and friends were already underway when Paul fell ill. The dinner was scheduled for late June, three weeks after his operation, and Paul insisted that we go ahead with it. When they learned of the circumstances, two of our dear New York friends, Arlyn and Ed Gardner, whom we had met in East Hampton in 1961, made the effort to fly out for the event. The dinner was bittersweet because everyone understood that Paul had terminal cancer. I'm so grateful that we had the chance to all be together. I have very warm memories of that evening.

Later that summer, after being by my side during the trauma of Paul's operation, my father fell ill and was hospitalized. In three weeks' time, he died of a brain tumor. He lived ninety-four years and had full possession of his faculties until the very end. It was devastating that, at a time when my mother needed me, I couldn't be there for her, nor could she be there to help me. It was one of those tragic life events over which we have no control and that test our mettle. Going to my father's funeral with my dying husband at my side was one of the most difficult things I ever had to do. Imagine sitting next to the man you love, who is himself under a death sentence, in a funeral parlor saying goodbye to another man you love. It was an aperçu of the pain that awaited when Paul died.

But my mother and I are strong. We had managed to survive the horrors of the Second World War, and we leaned on the strengths built surviving that ordeal. Her circumstances were different, given that she was twenty-five years younger than my father, and he had lived a long and full life. My situation was much more unusual—Paul was only fifty-four years old, in the prime of life. His illness had a profound effect on our friends, compelling them to reevaluate their own lives. They rallied around Paul and me in the most incredible manner. They supported us through the frequent visits to the hospital for chemotherapy and came to stay with Paul as needed to allow me to have time for myself. The last time we went out together in public was Mother's Day in May 1987 when we took my mother to lunch. Paul died on July 29, 1987.

We were also blessed to have our children near us throughout Paul's illness. Michèle was living and working in the Bay Area as a lawyer for Brown & Bain. When Paul was diagnosed, Gerald, who lived in Boston at the time, transferred to the San Francisco office of Bain & Company. While looking for a place for Gerald to live, I realized how gloomy our Sea Cliff neighborhood was in comparison to the sunnier clime of San Francisco's eastern neighborhoods. We decided to sell our house and move downtown to a neighborhood that would provide Paul with a much more cheerful and urbane environment. We found a wonderful condo at the Golden Gateway Commons, right in the heart of the Financial District and within walking distance to the Embarcadero and North Beach. I'll never forget when Paul asked me point-blank if moving in before he died would leave me with too many bad memories. I assured him that it was not a consideration. It was much more important for us to leave Sea Cliff and enhance his quality of life as much as possible.

In that awful year of Paul's illness, my daughter and I grew much closer. She took care of my mother and her grief at a time when I couldn't. Michèle's sexual identity ceased to mean anything to me. We began to relate to each other like two people who love each other very much and have come out of a challenge all the stronger for it.

CHAPTER 12

Paul's death was wrenching for me. We had been married thirty-three years and had never been apart except for two business trips—one that I took in the '60s and one in the '80s. Although I am a strong-willed and independent woman and Paul gave me a great deal of leeway in an era with clearly defined gender roles, we did everything together. I never went to a movie by myself, I never pursued a hobby that took me away from him other than exercise classes, and I never made plans that took me out of the house without him. He was a passionate football fan and I'm completely uninterested in any sport whatsoever, including the Olympics. But every Sunday during the season, I sat in the TV room with him reading the Sunday papers, never considering going off on my own for any purpose. Since age eighteen, I had lived my whole adult life with this man. Without him, I didn't know who I was. During Paul's illness, I kept my job at University High School, where the headmaster graciously accommodated my erratic schedule, and my colleagues were very supportive. After his death, I returned to work full time, grateful to have a place to go and things to do. That first year after his death, I couldn't bear the thought of spending the forthcoming holidays without Paul, so I went to visit my friend Naomi in Mexico for Thanksgiving, and joined my friends Lois and Danny in Saint Barts for Christmas. Those were the first times I traveled alone, and aside from desperately missing Paul, what I remember most is how challenging managing my suitcase was—those were the days before the wheelies.

Travel helped me learn to live without Paul. The summer of 1988, I spent three weeks with my French friends Dora and Jean-Claude. They lived in Pinel-Hauterive, a village in the southwest of France, in a beautiful, old farmhouse with a swimming pool, attached to a working orchard. They were nudists, so I joined them in that practice and have fond memories of that bucolic holiday. There's nothing like walking through an orchard at the end of the day, picking a ripe peach from a tree and biting into it while it's still warm from the sun. Dora, who was a lifelong heavy smoker, passed away at the age of seventy-four, stubbornly refusing to take care of her health. I visited them again in 1993 and in 2000 when Dora was mostly bedridden but still had the strength to cook delicious meals.

That same year, my New York friends Arlyn and Ed invited me to his sixty-fifth birthday bash on the Riviera. I stayed with them in a delightful villa they had rented. One hundred or so guests attended the festivities, which included an impressive fireworks display. Ed was truly beloved. He passed away in April 2020, and 350 people attended his Zoom memorial service. In addition to his extensive business connections, Ed dedicated over fifty years to Big Brothers Big Sisters of New York as both president and chair of its board of trustees. Our friendship started in 1961 and to this day, although a year or more can go by without talking to each other, Arlyn and I pick right up where we left off as soon as we get on the phone.

Just as our friends were exceptionally helpful during Paul's illness, they rallied around me after he passed. It's been said that when someone you love and with whom your life is so closely entwined dies, it takes an entire year to go through holidays, birthdays, and anniversaries to grieve. At the end of a year, either you go on and remake your life or you don't. I chose to remake my life. Life is too short not to start again. One of my dearest and most devoted friends, who saw me through the entire nightmare of Paul's illness and his death, lost her husband some twenty years later. She could not move on after her husband's death. Her health deteriorated, she had to give up her career, and she essentially drank herself to death. I tried every way I could to get her to acknowledge her problem and deal with it, but she refused. When she asked why I was the only one of her friends bullying her, I told her it was because I was Jewish and that all her other friends, in good Protestant fashion, stayed out of her business. She and I were polar opposites in how we handled widowhood. I refused to give up and just eke out the rest of my existence. Life is too precious to waste.

When I was ready to resume my life, my friends went out of their way to include me in social events. They introduced me to every age-appropriate single man they knew, and I dated more than I had done in my entire life. It's likely that I dated more than any other single woman in the city of San Francisco during the second year of my widowhood. I remember being at a restaurant where our lovely young waitress asked me whether my male companion and I were on a date. When I replied in the affirmative, she complained that she hadn't been on a date in the last six months.

I dated several members of the exclusive Bohemian Club, which was founded in 1872 by journalists, artists, and musicians and went on to admit businessmen and entrepreneurs as permanent members. It is the premier gathering place for almost exclusively rich white men, who play at rough living for two weeks in the summer. They belong to camps, each of which has its own version of a log cabin with few amenities in a wooded setting full of hiking trails and spectacular views. The members include luminaries in politics, academia, media, and entertainment. World-renowned leaders speak at the summer events including former presidents, heads of prestigious universities, members of the military, and diplomats. I heard fascinating and revelatory talks and enjoyed outstanding entertainment, not concerned at the time that the Bohemian Club did not admit women. Remember, this was 1988, long before the MeToo movement took hold.

The Bohemian Club is the ultimate meeting place for power players in all fields. For 150 years, it has provided a breeding ground for those who became leaders of various fields and who could always call on their fellow Bohemians, creating an incredible, tightly controlled network of movers and shakers who interacted once a year to renew relationships and explore new paths. Interestingly, this is leavened by the presence of artists, many of whom live entirely different lives from those of the rich and famous. At the Grove, they rub elbows, and the artists are given their due. They continue to contribute their talents, which are much appreciated.

As a widow, I literally became another person and felt entirely free. I tend to be hyperbolic in my passions and my pronouncements, and Paul had always acted as my anchor. He provided a counterbalance to my character traits. As I engaged in relationships with other men, I did not find anyone who complemented me the way Paul did. None of the introductions and subsequent dates led to a long-term relationship.

To expand my horizons, I signed up for a precursor of

eharmony. It was one of the first online dating services where members were filmed in an interview that was posted on the organization's site. Members could then contact one another if they liked what they saw in the interview. After four unsuccessful tries, I met Jack Stavert, a lawyer for AT&T who had recently moved to San Francisco. He was my intellectual equal and we began dating in earnest in 1990. We fell deeply in love, compatible because we were both independent, self-contained people. He proposed to me on Valentine's Day in 1992, and we were married in the beautiful home of my friends Jean and Jim, officiated by my daughter who, as a lawyer, was deputized for a day to perform the ceremony.

In 1992 I retired from my job at San Francisco University High School after twelve years as director of development. I had not one, not two, not three, but four retirement parties. One was held at the school with the teachers, parent volunteers, and members of the board of trustees. They presented me with a beautiful silver bowl with this inscription: "GISELE HUFF—With grateful appreciation from the UHS Parents Association—1992." The second party was a lunch at the home of a committee member of the Decorator Showcase, where I was given a silver Elsa Peretti bracelet from Tiffany. The third event was a dinner party at the home of Susan and Bill Oberndorf. The fourth was a large cocktail party at the home of Patti and Jerry Hume. No gold watch for me, but plenty of celebration and recognition!

After retiring, I sold my condo. Jack and I bought a house, which we remodeled, in the hills of San Rafael. It had a very large garden on the hillside as well as an extensive view. Jack was an avid gardener, so a plethora of flowers graced the house. We also grew tomatoes so plentifully that I gave out baskets of them. At the time we married, Jack knew very few people other than his business colleagues and became swept up in my social life. He made friends with the husbands of couples with whom Paul and I had been friends.

Jack's teenage daughter, Misa, lived with her mother in North Carolina. Misa was adrift and decided to come live in San Rafael. When she arrived, Misa was a very attractive, slight young woman who had no self-confidence, spoke in a barely audible voice, and wore shapeless clothes that hid her from the world. Jack bought her a car and set her up in a studio apartment while I used my connection with Dominican College, where I taught one course per semester pro bono, to get her a late registration. Within a few years she graduated and met a wonderful young man, much to our delight.

For the first two years of our relationship, Jack and I were like teenagers in love. For the next two years, we were very happy, but Jack was unable to accept that happiness and began a downward spiral. The happier we were, the more undeserving he felt. Something had occurred in his childhood that he could not forget or forgive himself for. He had demons that he couldn't defeat. We agreed to divorce in 1998. Because we were both very independent people with our own bank accounts, there was no question of community property. We meticulously divided what we held in common and went through the divorce process with a mediator who handled the paperwork and cost a mere $200. In retrospect, I realize I should have had the house reappraised to determine our respective shares because it had increased in value. Ultimately, though, it was for the best because it was much more important to me that we didn't get involved in a long, drawn-out, potentially contentious divorce.

While I was married to Jack, I became a grandmother for the first time. Gerald had married Judy, a woman he met at Harvard. The wedding was in September 1988 in the Los Altos backyard of Judy's parents, Joan and Jim Bliss. Jim has since passed away, but Joan and I remain close friends. The wedding was a bittersweet event because we still very much felt Paul's absence. Gerald and Judy settled in Berkeley and in December 1993, my grandson, Paul, was born, named after the grandfather he never knew. Judy is a doctor and because both she and Gerald had very demanding jobs, and because they loved to travel, I was called upon from time to time to take care of Paul. Jack and I set up a nursery in our San Rafael house. What a joy it was to have all the perks of motherhood without any of the responsibilities. Paul was a very sunny baby. My granddaughter, Jane, arrived fifteen months later.

That year Michèle, who worked at Sun Microsystems as the lawyer assigned to the development and release of Java, left the company, and moved to New Mexico to be with her partner at the time, Natalie, the writer. Michèle wanted to explore a writing career, but she eventually decided to return to the law, first hanging out her shingle as a sole practitioner for start-ups and then as a member of the law department of the University of New Mexico.

After my divorce, I moved to a condo in Peacock Gap, a community in San Rafael built around a golf course. My unit faced the course, and I adjusted to single life again—not a difficult transition, because for the last two years of my marriage, I was essentially alone. That was in February 2000, but by July, I returned to San Francisco, buying a condo in the very same complex where Paul and I had moved in 1986 and where I've lived ever since. I had thought that taking the ferry from Larkspur Landing, near San Rafael, to commute to the Ferry Building in San Francisco would be enjoyable, but driving to the terminal and then walking from the ferry to my office proved to be quite a challenge. Living in San Rafael added more than half an hour to the one-hour trip from San Francisco to where my mother lived in Cupertino, and as she was getting older, I felt I had to be closer to her.

At the age of sixty-two, I decided that I would never get romantically involved with a man again. I didn't want to get into a relationship with someone whose fragile ego I would have to cater to. As I imagined such a relationship, the cons outweighed the pros by a considerable margin. At that stage of my life, being alone was not a problem for me, and I continue to enjoy my solitude.

CHAPTER 13

Two years before our divorce and four years after my retirement, I was bored beyond words. I didn't have the temperament to become a volunteer, nor did I have a cause I was passionate about. So I decided to run for the California Sixth Congressional District seat in 1996. I was six months past my sixtieth birthday. I had never run for political office before, but when I moved from San Francisco to Marin County four years earlier, I was upset to learn that my congressional representative was Lynn Woolsey. She had been swept into office in 1992 on the wave of what was dubbed the "Year of the Woman," which included the election of Senator Barbara Boxer, who joined liberal Democratic Representative Nancy Pelosi.

Because of my progressive views on social issues, most people assumed I was a liberal. When Paul and I disclosed that we had voted for Barry Goldwater in the 1964 presidential election, our New York friends thought we were certifiable and worried about our mental health. As a fiscally conservative Libertarian, I strongly believed in pulling oneself up by one's bootstraps. It was hard for me to find a home, politically, so I had registered as an Independent in every election since I became a citizen in 1956.

I still get a thrill when I go into the voting booth. I've never missed an election, many of which took place before voting by mail was an option. Our children need to understand what a privilege it is to vote and how, to this day, people all over the world sacrifice their lives for the right to vote. It is not a privilege that should be taken for granted. The vote is one of the most precious rights that Americans have, a point I stressed on my campaign trail. I told audiences that on the wall of every middle and high school classroom in our nation should hang a picture of the lone Chinese student standing in front of the tank in Tiananmen Square in 1989.

When I realized that I was represented by Lynn Woolsey, I harked back to an argument Plato made in *The Republic* that the philosopher-king should govern his ideal society because no person wants to be ruled by someone lesser than herself. In my opinion, Representative Lynn Woolsey fell far short of the Platonic ideal. My first attempt to unseat her was in 1994 when I registered as a Republican so that I could work for Mike Nugent, her opponent. He lost the election, but I got a taste of political activism, and when Representative Woolsey was re-elected for the third time in November 1996, I was chomping at the bit to take action. The California Sixth Congressional District is heavily Democratic, but that did not deter me from throwing my hat in the ring.

When I started my campaign, I knew the importance of a candidate's backstory. As you know, mine is compelling, having survived the Holocaust and immigrating to the United States after the Second World War as an eleven-year-old child. I had truly lived the American Dream, and running for office was a way to give back. As is often the case with immigrants, my appreciation for the freedom and opportunity America offers is tangible in a way that differs from those born here, who tend to take these privileges for granted.

In spite of my lack of political experience, I had definitive ideas about how the country should be governed. Because of my age and my habit of cutting to the chase, I aimed for a national office rather than first run for a lower office. I viewed the federal government as bloated, ineffective, and woefully inadequate in spending the tax dollars it collected. At the same time, I was very aware of inequities and the chasm between the haves and have-nots. I remember being interviewed by the editorial board of the *Marin Independent Journal* and condemning a tax system that collected Social Security from minimum-wage workers while bond coupon-clippers received large sums that they did not need.

It takes a certain kind of self-confidence to decide to run for public office. Other than the Nugent campaign, I had never been involved in electoral politics. I had no connections to the Republican Party in the district, nor did I have a network of friends in Marin or Sonoma, the counties that comprised the sixth district at that time. I was definitely not in a position to self-finance, so as a first test of the viability of a run, I approached a San Francisco friend of mine to jump-start my fledgling campaign. Because we shared similar political views, he and his wife contributed the maximum allowed, $1,000 each, even though they couldn't vote for me because they lived outside my district, in San Francisco. With that $2,000 I purchased lists of registered voters as well as a computer-based fundraising tracking system that complied with the federal reporting requirements.

I put together a small staff and rented an office in Novato. One staffer was a young man who took a leave of absence from his job to be my campaign manager. He was a Democrat and had previously worked with Senator Dianne Feinstein. Because

I was already an unorthodox candidate—never having run for or held office before, of French origin, and adhering to that classic Libertarian combination of being fiscally conservative and socially liberal—I thought that having a Democrat for a campaign manager would establish my willingness to reach across the aisle. I question my choice now. I also thought that having a Democrat associated with my campaign in a heavily Democratic district would be an advantage, but it didn't turn out that way. My opponent, Lynn Woolsey, was part of the coterie of Democratic women in Congress, which included Senator Feinstein, and they had wide support. At one point, the young man running my campaign missed a deadline to purchase a listing for me in the Republican Party's voter guide. Instead, the name of my primary opponent appeared rather than mine. To this day, I wonder whether this was an oversight or whether it was sabotage.

Between the end of 1996 and the primary election on June 2, 1998, I raised $200,000. My approach was simple. I would visit with potential supporters and listen carefully to what they had to say. More often than not, we arrived at the values we shared: smaller, more efficient government; fiscal responsibility; and the preservation of freedom. I would then point out that, since they weren't willing to run for Congress themselves, it was incumbent upon them to contribute to the campaign of the like-minded person who was willing to.

I had set a goal of raising $1 million for the general election, which seems rather quaint these days, when congressional campaigns routinely cost millions of dollars. I outspent my Republican primary opponent ten to one, and I still lost that election. I attribute my loss partly to the fact that my name wasn't listed on the Republican slate flyer, which voters often take into the booth with them, and partly to the fact that my background may have been too "exotic" for the conservative Republicans I was trying to persuade.

The day of the primary, June 2, 1998, we gathered in my campaign office and tracked the results. It is interesting that I cannot remember the exact number of votes by which my Republican opponent beat me. Although I didn't win the election, the eighteen months I spent on the campaign trail were exhilarating and personally rewarding. I learned how to listen, how to articulate and defend my beliefs, and I encountered all kinds of people I never would have met otherwise.

Part II

CHAPTER 14

After I lost the Republican primary, I wanted to start a new career. Newly divorced and all revved up from my campaign, I was determined to find something meaningful to do with the rest of my life. After all, I was only sixty-two years old! I arranged a lunch with Sally Pipes, head of the Pacific Research Institute, a conservative think tank in San Francisco, hoping she could find a slot for me where I could use both my academic and political experience. She graciously pointed out that I was overqualified for the role I was interested in, but she informed me that Jerry Hume, with whom I had worked closely as a board member at University High School, was looking for an executive director for his family foundation, the Jaquelin Hume Foundation. I immediately reached out to Jerry, and he told me to send my résumé to the headhunter conducting a national search.

Out of the seven applicants for the job, the headhunter advocated for me and warned the trustees that given my personality, its policy of giving anonymously would not remain in place for long. The foundation was fiscally conservative and socially liberal, making me a good fit. Having known and worked with Jerry Hume for many years, I had already built trust with him. I was hired in November 1998. Thrilled with my new position, I moved into my office on the twenty-eighth floor of the iconoclastic Transamerica building. I had a fabulous view, and the foundation offered me an assistant, but I declined because for me, it would be much more stressful to worry about keeping that person occupied doing things that I was perfectly capable of doing myself.

This new chapter in my life was everything I could wish for—a full-time job where I could have an impact on the education of children. My position took me to national conferences in Denver, Chicago, Atlanta, Austin, New Orleans, New York, and many more cities across the nation. I thoroughly enjoyed the camaraderie with my colleagues and grantees at these conferences, and I developed strong relationships with many of the distinguished keynote speakers and session leaders.

In addition to traveling to conferences, I traveled quite a bit for pleasure. My position allowed twenty days of vacation a year, which I took full advantage of. In September 2001, while visiting my friend Naomi in Mexico, I was involved in a very bad car accident. We had driven Naomi's old car to a resort about four hours from her home in Mexico City. On our way back home, I hit a large, deep puddle in a pothole. I was going forty-five miles an hour; it was late afternoon after a rain shower, the sun glaring off the pavement. We went into a spin and veered perpendicularly, just barely avoiding a collision with a big truck. We hit a ditch, the car flipped over, and seat belts kept us in our seats, upside down. Although the landscape was barren and it seemed like not a soul was around, amazingly, people came to our aid. Naomi was removed from the passenger side uninjured. I knew that I had hurt my neck, and thanks to having watched several seasons of the television show *ER*, I knew I shouldn't be moved without a neck collar. I insisted we wait for the ambulance crew, which took an hour and a half to arrive. During that time, I remained upside down in the driver's seat, held in place by the seat belt. The paramedics took me to a local clinic, where they prepared me for the three-hour ambulance ride back to Mexico City. The pain was excruciating. I knew something was very wrong. It turned out that I had fractured my first and second vertebrae.

A few days after my return to San Francisco, my son drove me to be outfitted with a collar at UCSF and brought me back to my condo. After he left, I got a call telling me that the appointment I had been seeking with my PPO located in Marin County, from where I had recently moved, was available right then. I called a taxi, and when the doctor looked at the X-ray, he found that the vertebrae had moved six millimeters since the X-ray taken in Mexico. He immediately admitted me to the hospital, where I underwent an operation to install a halo that immobilized my head. It required drilling four holes in my skull, and I wore that contraption for three and a half months.

The hospital contacted my son and explained the situation. Gerald could not believe it, having just dropped me off at home a couple of hours previously, and he called his sister with the news, insisting that I was in one piece when he last saw me. It was during my stay in the hospital that 9/11 happened. I had already been fitted with the halo and was being trained on how to navigate with it when one of the therapists, who happened to be in the room when President George W. Bush was on screen, said, "I hope he dies." This was in very liberal Marin County, but it shocked me and I berated her, first, for such a callous statement when the country needed its leadership more than ever, and second, because she had no idea what my politics were, and to express herself that way in front of a patient was unacceptable.

It was important to keep the sites of the screws that held the halo steady free of infection, so they needed to be swabbed daily. Because of the awkward way the halo was positioned, it was not possible for me to reach the sites, but I was able to get a young woman who provided full-time care to a neighbor to stop by every day when she was walking the dog. When the alternative is not an option, there is always a solution to the problem, in this case involving a $25-per-week tip and the possibility of it fitting into her schedule with no interference with her full-time job.

Because I'm a very independent person, I found wearing the halo quite challenging. It didn't just limit movement of my neck; it limited my entire life. I could do very few things on my own. For instance, I couldn't look down, which meant that I couldn't leave the house by myself, because I couldn't even negotiate a curb. Luckily, the foundation was very accommodating. They arranged for me to work from home and for transport to doctor appointments. I could take shallow baths but not showers because the halo rested in a heavy plastic vest lined with lamb's wool. So every weekend, Judy, my daughter-in-law, who is a doctor, would come to my home and wash my hair as I lay on the chaise longue on my patio with my head hanging over the rim. I'll forever be grateful to Judy for her care. She's a very giving person, always going above and beyond. We have a wonderful relationship, disproving the old canards about mothers-in-law.

Even strangers offered their help. For instance, I couldn't go to the hairdresser, so whenever I went out in public, I wore an artfully arranged scarf to cover my hair. I always found someone willing to help me reach around the halo to tie the scarf on the back of my head. When I traveled to Washington, DC, for a conference, halo and all, one of the young women who worked for the sponsoring organization offered her help.

During that trip, at the San Francisco airport, I ran into a colleague from the Hoover Institution, who could not get over my being there. I explained I had to attend a very important board meeting. This was before the advent of virtual participation, and I made it my business to use whatever means necessary, including the wheelchair service that airlines provide for disabled or elderly passengers. It is my belief that when you agree to serve on a board, you have a responsibility to attend the meetings during which your fiduciary and policy-making duties take place.

During the last three weeks of wearing the halo, the screws holding the rods to my skull slowly shifted, giving rise to excruciating pain. I had seldom used painkillers, forgoing them even after various serious medical procedures, but in this case, I had to take them every four hours, even during the night.

I survived the ordeal and regained full motion in my neck after several weeks of intensive therapy. The experience taught me how dependent we are on each other and how rewarding it is when the people around you rally to help in challenging circumstances.

CHAPTER 15

A couple of months after I had started working at the foundation in November 1998, the trustees and I met with a facilitator to bring focus to the foundation's philanthropic activities. The board consisted of the widow of Jaquelin "Jack" Hume, his two sons, and the organization's lawyer. In keeping with Jack Hume's wishes, the foundation made grants primarily to national nonprofit organizations supporting small government, free-market ideas, and local civic organizations. For several years before his death, as CEO of the foundation, Jack Hume made the funding decisions on his own. After his death, his longtime administrative assistant was given the task of organizing the disbursement of funds, but it fell to the board members to decide how to allocate them. His sons, Jerry and George Hume, were very busy running the family-owned company, and the fund allocation process devolved into a mind-boggling, week-long parade of nonprofit organizations making presentations. That is why the board decided to bring on an executive director with the credentials and expertise to sift through the proposals, summarize them, make informed recommendations, and establish knowledgeable relationships with grantees.

Shortly after I was hired, and with the help of the facilitator who led us in a discussion of how the foundation should proceed, the trustees agreed to focus on education reform in the kindergarten through high school (K–12) space. Jack Hume had always been a supporter of education reform, and his son Jerry Hume, who was appointed by Governor Pete Wilson to the California State Board of Education, was passionate about it himself. And so was I.

At the time, education reform was nothing new. As a nation, we've been grappling with the issue for four decades. In 1983, President Reagan commissioned a report called *A Nation at Risk*. It was a scathing indictment of our education system, which the report asserted was swimming "in a rising tide of mediocrity." Among the most memorable phrases in the report is this one: "If an unfriendly foreign power had attempted to impose on America the mediocre educational performance that exists today, we might well have viewed it as an act of war."

The report was a wake-up call that launched an education reform movement that sadly has not yet succeeded. Millions of underserved children, like my classmates in the South Bronx in 1947 and gifted children with unrecognized talents, are being shortchanged every day in school. I'm shocked by the continued lack of attention K–12 education receives. Among the endless primary debates in the Republican Party in 2016 and in the Democratic Party in 2020, hardly a mention was made of how crucial education is to a functioning society. The education system was originally designed to produce material prosperity by teaching people to fit into the growing economy and to understand the functioning of their government at a basic level. Although over a century old, this system is still in place and it's failing miserably. In today's world, our children need to learn critical thinking, and critical thinking is absent from curricula, as is civics, a subject no longer taught in public schools. To prepare our children for this rapidly changing world, we need to shift from an emphasis on teaching to an emphasis on learning. We need to make each individual child the focus of education, which, as I will get into later, is possible if we incorporate technology into the curriculum.

As I write, I am disappointed by the major changes in education proposed by the Biden administration. The administration proposes extending schooling by two years of prekindergarten and two years of community college. But extended schooling will not make a difference if it's just four extra years of the same-old same old. We need to improve the whole enterprise of educating our children. Education is the fundamental basis for our democracy, and in its current form, it does not prepare our children to be responsible, productive citizens. As Thomas Jefferson wrote, "I know no safe depository of the ultimate powers of society, but the people themselves: and if we think them not enlightened enough to exercise their control with a wholesome discretion, the remedy is, not to take it from them, but to inform their discretion by education."

When masses of immigrants came to the United States at the beginning of the twentieth century, a majority were illiterate and never learned to speak English. Public schools transformed these immigrants' children into educated citizens who contributed mightily to the innovations of the twentieth century and went on to become the Greatest Generation. Integrating the children of immigrants within one generation was the great achievement of the K–12 education system and a testament to the power of education. That is no longer the case.

Of course, the world was a much simpler place then. But the upheaval of the pandemic presents an opportunity for us to think differently about education. It's time to stop trying desperately to cram the moribund premises of a twentieth-century system into a twenty-first-century paradigm. Being in lockdown has revealed to parents the mediocrity of the system. It isn't only the woefully underserved schools that are being shortchanged. The entire public-school system suffers from outdated practices and the lack of forward thinking. This pandemic has shown that we need to implement personalized learning and move from an industrial-training model to a critical-thinking model.

When we decided to focus on K–12 education, the foundation embarked on a strategy that funded organizations engaged in challenging the education establishment. Most of our grants addressed policy and, unusually at the time, were earmarked for operations rather than for specific projects. Let me explain by first making a distinction between what I consider charity and what I consider philanthropy. Philanthropy tackles big societal problems by approaching them at the systemic level, whereas charity tackles societal problems by approaching them at an individual level. For instance, donating to the United Way or Boys & Girls Clubs or your local religious institution is charity. Your contributions may well have a significant impact on individual lives, and that is certainly laudable. But it doesn't—and it will never—change the world. Even much larger contributions such as the $100 million that John Walton and Ted Forstmann donated to establish the Children's Scholarship Fund in 1998 served just 40,000 children out of the 1.25 million who applied. In the following twenty-three years, the Children's Scholarship Fund has given scholarships to 185,000 children out of the one billion (with a *b*) children who attended public schools in that time.

When the Hume Foundation decided to invest in education reform, we identified national organizations whose missions aligned with ours and gave them operating funds to pursue research and advocacy efforts to promote the school choice movement. This was a longtime focus of conservatives who, taking their lead from the economist Milton Friedman's theory, wanted to establish a voucher system where parents would be given the public moneys allocated to education and would be free to spend it at the school of their choice. We left it up to the organizations we worked with to decide how best to spend the funds rather than restricting them to a particular project.

This is unusual since only 16 percent of foundation grants go to operational expenses. Big bureaucratic foundations usually decide where they want to make investments and then find nonprofit organizations to help them do just that. Unfortunately, even with high-caliber program officers who oversee various portfolios, these foundations are not in the trenches. The hoops that grantees must jump through, starting with tailoring their proposals to the foundations' views of the problem, are onerous—not to mention the reporting required. In one case I know of, the recipient spent sixty-eight hours completing the necessary reporting.

Of course, people have every right to dispose of their money as they see fit, bearing in mind that these funds are tax-exempt. To retain that status, private foundations must distribute 5 percent of their revenue every year to nonprofit organizations with a charitable or educational purpose, and that figure includes "reasonable and necessary" expenses (which might cover a retreat in Hawaii for the trustees and the staff). The foundations' trustees are the sole determinants of how the funds are spent as long as they meet the guidelines of the IRS.

It's much more sensible and efficient for foundations to

identify nonprofits on the front lines of the causes the foundation supports, assess their performance, and then grant the nonprofits operational funds to use to achieve the mutual goals rather than project-based giving according to the foundation's own views. Occasionally, foundations should also act as venture capitalists and, like my modus operandi, "throw spaghetti at the wall." In my career, I made several breakthrough small grants that earned me the sobriquet of the queen of ROI (return on investment). More about that later.

To go back to the development of the Hume Foundation's mission, it became clear that, since education is essentially a state matter, we had to work at the state level to pass laws allowing vouchers, the opening of charter schools, education tax credits, and education savings accounts. To do so, we turned to state-based, free-market think tanks to educate legislators about the need to dramatically expand opportunities for parents of underserved children to choose for themselves what school their children should attend.

It's important to note that none of our efforts nor those of the organizations we funded were aimed at reforming the curriculum. Instead, we were trying to institutionalize the ability of many more children to exit the public-school system. Our goal was to use market forces like competition for customers to establish a system of educational governance and funding that empowered parents and was aimed at ultimately improving the educational product. School choice would mean that parents would have the option of using vouchers to put toward the tuition of their school of choice, allowing them to withdraw their children from the public-school system if they chose to. The vouchers would be paid for with tax dollars, and that typically amounted to less than the cost of educating children in local public schools. Another approach we supported was more indirect with charter schools operating within the public-school system but granted more freedom in their teaching methodology and curriculum. These charter schools are tuition-free and cannot have restrictive entrance requirements. If they are oversubscribed, admission is by lottery. In 1991, Minnesota had passed the nation's first charter school law in this model.

Institutionalizing the ability for children to exit the public-school system was Herculean work. We were challenging the status quo where even changes deemed desirable by its advocates were extremely difficult to implement. Battles ensued and continue to rage on today. A voucher law passed in Utah was soon rescinded by a referendum placed on the ballot. A charter school law that passed in Washington State was ruled unconstitutional by the Washington State Supreme Court. I found this one step forward, two steps back experience extremely frustrating. But another concern began to nag at me—the math didn't add up.

At that time, there were about 450,000 children who used some type of voucher and an estimated three million children attending charter schools. Every year, on average, some fifty-five million children attend school in the United States. By combining students who attend private, parochial, or charter schools, that's 7 percent of students that are educated outside of district public schools. This is a dreadfully small percentage, after more than twenty-five years of efforts to reform education and billions of dollars invested by foundations to make it happen.

As an example, KIPP (which stands for the Knowledge Is Power Program) launched twenty-seven years ago and now has 270 charter schools in operation throughout the United States, educating around 110,000 children. KIPP is a flagship organization that started a no-excuses model in underserved inner-city and rural schools. KIPP put to rest the idea that some children can't learn and demonstrated that when high expectations are set, all children will strive to meet them. I give KIPP much credit for helping to shift the national education debate from an emphasis on inputs and compliance to one that emphasizes outcomes and student success.

But if it took nearly three decades to arrive at that 7 percent figure and cost billions, and if we optimistically halve the number of years and double the number of charter schools created, it means that twelve years from now, only 14 percent of America's children will be attending these schools. Meanwhile, a majority of children currently attending district public schools are children of color, the most underserved demographic. This is a crisis of immense urgency. Our current pace of reform will leave millions of children behind.

As I came to grips with the math and the daunting challenges in taking on the education establishment, I had an epiphany. In 2005, I attended the annual conference of the Education Commission of the States, an organization that brings together governors, state education commissioners, legislators, district leaders, and other nonofficial stakeholders. Because the Hume Foundation supported the organization, I was invited to join a small group to meet with one of the keynote speakers at a private luncheon. That speaker was Clayton Christensen, the Kim B. Clark Professor of Business Administration at the Harvard Business School. In preparation for the meeting, we were asked to read the sequel to his first, seminal book, *The Innovator's Dilemma*. That book, *The Innovator's Solution*, changed my worldview.

How, you may ask, could a book written by a business school professor about disruptive innovation in the corporate marketplace possibly influence an education policy wonk with a PhD in political philosophy? Before I explain, let me say that the experience taught me that one never knows where enlightenment will come from. That's why I am always open to new ideas and seek to incorporate them in my worldview when they prove to be valuable. I've also found that when I share dilemmas with other people, they often offer a solution that I had not thought of on my own.

To go back to disruptive innovation, let me give you a quick case study example of how Christensen describes the concept. In the 1950s, RCA produced an amazingly authentic listening experience for music lovers like Paul and me. We purchased an expensive RCA stereo system that required a room at least fifteen feet wide to install the speakers at a proper distance for maximum fidelity. The system ran on vacuum tubes that needed to be changed frequently and created a sound almost as good as that experienced in a concert hall. As you can imagine, the stereo system was very expensive and out of reach for most—including teenagers, who could not afford such a system. And even if their parents could afford it, it's unlikely they'd let their kids play rock and roll music on the deluxe RCA stereo system.

The Japanese company we now know as Sony saw an opportunity here. They didn't invent the transistor radio, but they commercialized it, making the radios widely available starting in 1954. RCA was so focused on their high-end stereo system that it didn't occur to them that they were ignoring a large portion of the marketplace. Sony stepped in and began mass producing the transistor radio. Customers loved the radios because they were cheap and portable. Teenagers could listen to Elvis Presley whenever and wherever they wanted. People who couldn't afford even the cheapest of RCA's systems were delighted to have access to Sony's radios. By disrupting the status quo and meeting the demand of customers, Sony's success with the transistor radio led to the eventual demise of prohibitively expensive vacuum-tube-reliant stereo systems.

We need more disruptors like this in education, but a big problem innovators face in bureaucratic systems is that the culture prevents disruptive ideas from taking hold. This is true in K–12 education. Teachers are trapped in existing practices and protocols. The pacing guide dictates what is taught and for how long, no matter what an individual student needs. Success is measured not by what students learn but by how well they perform on tests. Teachers have little opportunity to collaborate on a framework within which to innovate, to improve, and to course correct. Teachers are solely responsible for educating children, but they have very little control over the curriculum and, paradoxically, there is no way to monitor how they teach once they close the classroom door.

The public-school curriculum is designed to mold the children into widgets that will fit into what President Eisenhower dubbed the military-industrial complex, which has grown exponentially since he spoke of it in his farewell address in January 1961. It's no surprise that the public-school day is regulated by bells, that desks are arranged in a row, and that young children are taught to walk and stand in lines. It's no surprise that schooling (which is done *to* children as opposed to learning, which is done *by* children) is punitive—failure is stigmatized rather than accepted as a step toward success. It's no surprise that students are motivated by competition rather than collaboration.

It became very clear to me that education reform would never provide children what they need to meet the tremendous challenges of the twenty-first century. What's needed is not reform, but rather a transformation. We need to look at education through the lens of the disruptive innovation that Clayton Christensen had advanced.

CHAPTER 16

An important part of the reform movement was the launch of charter schools. These public schools have to meet the performance criteria of traditional schools but are run by a board independent of the school district. At the time there was an uneasy alliance between the school choice movement and the charter school proponents; these groups hold opposite ideological positions, although they have the same goal of delivering quality education to America's children by going outside the traditional public-school system. Because of the pandemic, the entire K–12 space has changed drastically. Lockdowns challenged an ill-prepared online learning system, which is an important part of transforming the educational experience. The battles that are being fought around schooling are now much more ideological than those that involved school choice and charter school proponents. It's hard for me to see in what direction we are going to go, but the need to transform the way and what our children learn has never been more urgent.

In general, charter schools were championed by people like Bill Gates and Jerry Brown, when he was mayor of Oakland.

School choice was championed by more conservative groups such as my foundation, which also funded the Foundation for Teaching Economics, an organization that the late Jack Hume started in 1975. Milton Friedman was a member of its board, and as the executive director of the foundation, I sat in on the board meetings as well as attended the annual dinners. In 1955, Milton Friedman had authored a foundational paper proposing a shift in funding and governance mechanisms for public K–12 schools, suggesting that parents be awarded tuition vouchers that they could use to pay for private-sector education services for their children, rather than relying on government-provided services. I had one-on-one debates with Milton on many occasions—me coming to the table as a former administrator in a rigorous private school, versus him, a world-renowned, Nobel Prize–winning conservative economist. Although at that time I agreed with his theories, I argued against his contention that if all the public schools closed and parents were given vouchers to send their children to schools of their choice, demand would generate the supply necessary to provide quality education to all students. Knowing how difficult it is to start a good school and to maintain a level of excellence, I argued that in education, supply and demand did not operate the way it did in any other segment of the marketplace. Needless to say, I didn't convince him, and he didn't convince me, either.

My experiences as the director of development at San Francisco University High School and my relationship with the likes of Ray Dolby and Mimi Haas held me in good stead in these conversations. Milton was a delightful, witty, brilliant man and we were both Jewish. As I mentioned before, being Jewish is not merely a religious affiliation (for me, it is not at all, since I don't practice) but a tribal one. We were very comfortable with each other. He never condescended to me, but more to the point, I didn't expect him to. I felt very secure in my knowledge of how schools work and how little market principles play in a monolithic industry almost entirely impervious to innovation. The policies Milton championed may have given parents more opportunities to choose their children's school, but in my view, it was not realistic. Without a different curriculum, those schools would not be any better at preparing students for the twenty-first century.

As I became deeply involved in the school choice movement, I had amazing opportunities to meet other brilliant people in the field. Some of these people were very conservative, and although my worldview has changed drastically in recent years, these relationships remain very valuable to me, both professionally and personally. I am very passionate in my views, but I'm also a good listener and I pay close attention to other people's perspectives—often I see a truth in their perspective that leads me to adjust mine.

My dear friend Bill Oberndorf, who had been my campaign finance chair when I ran for Congress, was the head of the American Education Reform Foundation, which was later renamed the Advocates for School Choice. He ran the organization with the late John Walton. By coincidence, when I had applied for the job with the Hume Foundation, I had also interviewed with Bill and John for the position of director of development for their organization.

The Advocates for School Choice aimed to promote all aspects of school choice. Every year it sponsored a conference for proponents and supporters in Jackson Hole, Wyoming, where John lived. John was an heir of the Walmart family fortune and the humblest billionaire I have ever met. I had many occasions to talk with him over the years, but most memorable was when I sat next to him at dinner and had his undivided attention for the duration of the meal. Here was a man who lived in a small western state far removed from inner cities, their pathologies, and the dismal public education system in those areas. He could do anything he wanted with his enormous fortune, and he chose to devote himself to giving children the educational opportunities they deserve.

John was a real-life Gary Cooper, or at least he was the embodiment of the characters Gary Cooper portrayed. He even looked like the actor. His quiet generosity of spirit led him to the path he had chosen. An avid outdoorsman and a risk-taker, John died when he crashed in a plane he had built from a kit. His death at the age of fifty-nine was a great loss for the school choice movement. I remember learning about the accident in the middle of the afternoon and leaving my office in tears, raging against him all the way home for having deprived us of more of his contributions.

Another adventure associated with this conference was that Bill invited me to fly with him to Wyoming on a private jet. I had flown on an early model in Mexico in the 1960s, but this was an entirely different experience and not the last time that I enjoyed it. Years later, when I decided to attend the Aspen Ideas Festival (an annual conference that brings together the American elite of the financial, political, and media worlds), Bill and his wife, Susan, invited me to stay with them and to join them on the flight to Aspen. At the last moment, their schedule changed, but they arranged for me to make the flight anyway. On the day of, a limousine picked me up and took me to the private airport, where there were no security measures—you just showed your ID and the staff took care of your luggage—and I boarded a jet large enough to accommodate eight passengers and with a flight attendant on board. There I was in solitary splendor, thinking back to where I came from and how magical it was for me to find myself in this moment. When we landed and Bill came to pick me up, I gave him a big hug and told him I felt like Cinderella.

Bill is that rare philanthropist who not only writes very generous checks to the causes he supports, but also devotes his time and energy to promoting them. He has been a school choice advocate for more than twenty-five years and has led national organizations that support it. He has served as the chair of the board of the University of California, San Francisco (UCSF), which raised hundreds of millions of dollars during his tenure. He is a genuine person with a gift for empathizing with people from all walks of life. He fits the old-fashioned sobriquet "a prince of a fellow." In every circumstance where he could be of help to me, starting with raising money for my congressional run in 1996, he has been stalwart in his support. It is a privilege to be his friend.

John and Bill were just two of the luminaries I spent time with at conferences. One year, I went on a hike with now Senator Cory Booker, who at that time was running for mayor of Newark. He was a proponent of school choice, Newark having one of the lowest-performing school systems in New Jersey. I remember thinking that he could well be the first Black president of the United States, but President Obama beat him to it. When I met him, I found Cory to be very charismatic and as passionate about the cause as an old-fashioned preacher. When he became mayor, Cory continued to promote school choice, but changed his tune when he became a senator, much to the chagrin of the conservatives in the movement who had supported him even though he was a Democrat.

When Advocates for School Choice was renamed the American Federation for Children, Betsy DeVos became the chair of the board and, of course, several years later became the secretary of education in the Trump administration. Betsy is an earnest person who, when I knew her, was totally devoted to the school choice movement and to the welfare of children. She and her husband, Dick DeVos, were the main sponsors of the 2000 ballot initiative to establish school vouchers in Michigan. The initiative lost by a vote of 69 percent against and 31 percent for. The DeVos family and other supporters had invested $14 million in the initiative, twice what their opponents spent. Voucher initiatives in California—Proposition 174 in 1993, and Proposition 38 in 2000—also were defeated by similar margins.

As she was a lifelong supporter of school choice with no experience or connection to public schools, it was no surprise that during her tenure as secretary of education, Betsy DeVos championed school choice. Conservatives' long-standing belief is that public schools are "government schools," and like most government enterprises, public schools are viewed by conservatives as inefficient and unresponsive; they haven't delivered an adequate education for many of the nation's children. In addition, many conservatives believe that public schools are negatively influenced by radical ideas, that they are a hotbed of brainwashing of vulnerable children.

I remember a conversation I had with Betsy in the hallway of a conference hotel when I was advocating investing in the burgeoning blended-learning movement, which involves introducing technology as an integral part of the curriculum, as I will explain in more detail later. At some point, she showed me an adorable picture of her two granddaughters in which the toddler held the baby's finger to help her swipe across an iPad. "Betsy," I said, "this proves my point. Technology is ubiquitous and will only become more so as your grandchildren grow up, so now is the time to harness it to make sure that they are prepared for the twenty-first century." As with many of my efforts with ideologically committed people, I didn't get anywhere, but I'm grateful I had the opportunity to exchange ideas with her.

I also had the opportunity to work with the Koch Foundation. At that time, they were intent on countering the heavily liberal bent of academia and on challenging the government's regulatory regime, which they believed stifled the American entrepreneurial spirit. Because of my relationship with the Hume Foundation and my work in the education space, I was invited to the Koch Foundation's conferences. At one of those conferences, I made a presentation about blended learning featuring Michael Horn and Susan Patrick, the CEO and president of iNACOL (International Association for K-12 Online Learning). I had several conversations with Charles Koch, a Libertarian bent on giving conservatism a voice in the American dialogue. He's an imposing man both physically and intellectually, but—obviously, since he allowed me to feature my pet project at his conference—he had an open mind and he listened to me.

In 2020, Koch co-wrote with Brian Hooks a book entitled *Believe in People: Bottom-Up Solutions for a Top-Down World*, in which he expresses disappointment with some of the candidates his organization funded who ultimately didn't support the Libertarian ideology when they became legislators. This has been viewed as a mea culpa of sorts to reposition the Koch name while, all along, the organization is sponsoring voter suppression efforts that would solidify its hold on state capitals, congressional seats, and even Supreme Court appointments. When I met Koch more than a decade ago, I was a lifelong Libertarian and in lockstep with his view that government is too big, too expensive, too inefficient, and too regulated. The free market had given us prosperity, and its tenets were far more beneficial to the commonweal than the bureaucratic behemoth that the American government had become. At the time I applauded Charles and the efforts of his foundation. But since the Great Recession in 2008 to 2009, my perspective has shifted 180 degrees, and I view Charles and many other people I met in that phase of my life as being oblivious to the damage that the free market has done and continues to do.

When I look back at my time in the school-reform movement and my involvement with mostly Republican, conservative, and Libertarian organizations, I can see that I overlooked the part of their agenda that specifically identified the teachers' unions as the enemy. They attributed much of the failure of the education system to the unions' protection of incompetent teachers, their inflexible control over working conditions in public schools, and their constant demand for more money. Some of the reformers used their professed concern for underserved children as a weapon to defeat the unions, whereas others were genuinely in the fray for the sake of those children.

I have been exposed to all sides of the argument and remain deeply committed to the need to create a twenty-first-century educational system that will prepare our children to meet its daunting challenges.

CHAPTER 17

In 2009, I lost my mother. Two months shy of her ninety-fourth birthday, she died in my arms in a coma as I told her over and over in French that I was there with her. Nine years earlier she had moved to a retirement community, where she became the queen bee of the ladies who played mahjong, poker, and trivia games. But in the last years of her life, her health deteriorated, and she had to move into an assisted living arrangement, where she was very lonely and unhappy. It was a very impersonal facility, and she had difficulty finding friends there. She couldn't live with me because I traveled often for my job, and I could not physically manage her. This is the dilemma of older people (I was sixty-nine years old at the time) who have even more elderly parents. Once, when I spent the night at her apartment before she moved to the retirement community, she fell, and I could not manage to pick her up. I had to call 911. After one of several hospital stays, she and I decided she should move into a board and care facility, an option that was more suited to her increasing lack of mobility and would provide her with more personal care.

Fortunately, we found her a home close to my condo, which allowed me to see her at least twice a week and take her shopping or out to lunch on the weekend. This facility had five or six residents and three attentive, kind, and efficient staff members. I couldn't have asked for better care. My mother retained her faculties until the very end, even continuing to manage her finances. I shared everything with her about my life and would describe to her at length my achievements and disappointments in my work. She did so much to encourage me in my pursuit of education reform. She asked probing questions that made me refine my take on experiences, and she praised my ability to collaborate with people from all backgrounds.

As part of the effort to enhance the lives of their clients, the facility subscribed to a program, Art With Elders, to teach painting through a nonprofit organization called Eldergivers. At the age of eighty-nine, my mother started to copy the works of the impressionists and produced more than a hundred watercolors amazingly faithful to the originals—a remarkable achievement for someone who had never held a paintbrush before.

My sister, Diana, made a recording of my mother recounting her life when she was ninety. When she died, I transcribed that recording word for word except for syntax corrections and published a book that featured dozens of her paintings. The foreword was written by the author Natalie Goldberg, my daughter's ex-partner. Natalie saw my mother as an extraordinary person and greatly admired her. The title of the book is *Berthe Baron: Reflections of an Ordinary Woman*, and it served as a fundraiser for Eldergivers. It was a labor of love for me, but my mother would probably have been embarrassed to have so much attention paid to her life; she was a very self-effacing person.

One of the many wonderful memories of my unusually

close relationship with my mother was the trip we took to Cabo San Lucas, Mexico, to celebrate the millennial New Year in 2000. I rented a villa with a swimming pool in a lovely resort right on the beach. I invited Gerald and Judy and my grandchildren, Paul and Jane, as well as Michèle and her partner at the time, Natalie. One evening, we had made a reservation at a restaurant that we thought was close to our resort, and we started to walk toward it along the beach. It turned out to be much farther than we thought, and we practically had to carry my mother as we got closer. She was not one for exercise and at the age of eighty-four, not in good physical shape. But she was a witty, engaging woman and was always able to make the best of the worst situations.

By that time my daughter and I enjoyed a very close relationship as well. Michèle is a wonderful traveling companion, and we have visited the Middle East, China, India, and Southeast Asia together. I cherish my relationship with Michèle and her partner, Terri, and I so enjoy traveling with my children and their families. We all have wanderlust. We've visited Italy, Mexico, Jamaica, and Las Vegas, and took a driving trip through Scotland, Ireland, and England. I also took my grandchildren, Paul and Jane, on cruises in the Caribbean, Greece, and Turkey.

You may wonder how I can afford all these treks. When Paul died, I had to manage my finances for the first time. I maintained the very conservative investment strategy that Paul had followed. Most of my investments are in bonds, except for an annuity that has grown ten times and whose principal I have never touched. When it comes to money, I am risk averse, which is why I don't like to gamble. My one indulgence has always been to travel. As soon as Paul's company went public, we did a five-week driving tour of Europe with our children, who were five years and eleven years old at the time.

Our goal was to eat at as many three-star Michelin restaurants as possible and to see world-renowned sites, including the grotto at Lascaux before it closed to the public. It was an amazing experience to see cave paintings fifteen thousand to seventeen thousand years old and to imagine our ancestors creating them as they struggled for survival.

Like many New Yorkers, we sought to escape the brutal, seemingly endless winter weather either at Christmas or at the February school break by escaping to Barbados, Martinique, and Antigua. But mostly, we visited our friends Naomi and Henry in Mexico, where he had the use of his company's private plane. It was an incredible privilege to get a bird's-eye view of the ruins of Chichén Itzá from above and visit other archaeological sites. We loved Mexico and the warmth of the people there.

After Paul's death, I continued to enjoy traveling. In 2015, I decided to take the plunge and spent almost $100,000 on a trip around the world in a private jet with *National Geographic*. This had long been an item on my bucket list. It gave me the opportunity to visit places that I never would have seen, such as Easter Island. What especially appealed to me was that out of the eleven sites included in the tour, I had already seen five, and *National Geographic* offered an exciting alternate in each instance. Instead of Machu Picchu, I took a trip to the coast, where a pre-Inca civilization thrived in an amazing adobe city. Only six out of the seventy-four people on the tour went to that site. I had a similar experience in India. I had already been to Agra, so with one other traveler and a driver and a guide, I visited Fatehpur Sikri, a city that had been the capital of the province before Agra and built by the same king. On our way through the countryside, we saw several gatherings of people being addressed by men on makeshift stages. I was fascinated to learn that it was election season, and since most people in those areas are illiterate, candidates had to visit each town in person to campaign.

Traveling with *National Geographic* offered many advantages. We flew only during daylight hours, which eliminated jet lag; we stayed at five-star hotels where we received first-class treatment; and we never had to deal with the hassle of passport clearance and commercial airline regulations. I was amazed at how renowned and respected *National Geographic* is. To give you an example, on our flight to Tibet we had to land in China first, but the night before, the Chinese government denied us entry. In the space of a few hours, our group leaders were able to arrange an impromptu visit to Bhutan, an amazing country with 763,000 inhabitants, whose national measure is not the Gross Domestic Product as it is for most nations, but the Gross National Happiness of its people. It is a very quaint corner of the world, and we were granted an audience with the Queen Mother of Bhutan, with all the panoply that entailed. Three other highlights of the trip for me were joining an indigenous dance troop on stage in Samoa, riding a camel in the marvel that is Petra, and flying a few hundred feet above Kilimanjaro.

Seeing such sights has brought me much joy, as has sharing my wealth with friends and family and those in need. My comfortable financial situation made it possible for me to pay for a caregiver for twenty years for a family member stricken with multiple sclerosis, who was bedridden and could not afford care. I was able to buy a mobile home and pay the association dues for a couple of friends who had fallen on hard times in their retirement. I'm not telling you this to pat myself on the back; I'm telling you this so that you understand the values I embrace. Not helping when I'm able to do so is not an option for me.

Although I'm very comfortable in my own skin and I don't need the approval of others, I am very sensitive to the needs of my fellow human beings. I always find something positive to say before offering constructive criticism. I learned that skill from my mother, who was very perceptive. When I shared my ideas with her, she didn't pull punches. She would challenge my ideas, but she did it lovingly, which taught me that it is always easier to achieve your goals when you listen to other people. When I talk with customer service people on the phone because of problems I encounter, I always thank them for their courtesy and help, and it almost always leads to satisfactory results. It costs nothing to be warm and caring, and the return on investment is very satisfying. If only more people practiced kindness, we would all be much happier, and the world would be a much better place.

CHAPTER 18

In 2005 I met Clayton Christensen, which led to the second phase of my career. As you'll remember from earlier in the book, Christensen spoke at the conference of the Education Commission of the States. After a lunch we both attended, I gave him my card and told him how impressed I was with his disruptive view of the education industry, words that I had never thought of applying to my work. I mentioned that the foundation I worked for would potentially be interested in promoting his ideas when he published them.

I began to channel Clay in conversations with colleagues and during Q&A sessions at national conferences. I asserted that technology needs to be an integral part of the school curriculum. I argued that the education industry was woefully behind all other industries. We needed a learning model that would afford teachers access to technological tools that had become ubiquitous in other industries. Every time I opened my mouth, my colleagues' eyes would glaze over. They knew that when I raised my hand (I always sat in the front row and was usually the first to raise my hand), I was going to wax poetic about technology. I was so well known for asking the first question that once, at a Hoover Institution meeting of their K-12 Education Task Force, Checker Finn, the president of the Thomas B. Fordham Institute, saw my hand shoot up at the end of the presentation and said outright that he wouldn't call on me first. At another event, I remember asking the then Secretary of Education Arne Duncan after his presentation where we would find people to deliver the "high-quality" prekindergarten education he advocated for when we already had a big problem properly staffing K–12 classrooms. In that instance as in many others, attendees came up to me at the end of the session and pointed out that he didn't answer my question.

Clay had sent me a précis of the book he intended to publish about disrupting education. He planned to write a lengthy first chapter explaining his revolutionary view and then have K–12 education luminaries write individual pieces about their view of disruptive innovation. I pushed back on two counts: 1) compendia are a dime a dozen, gathering dust in warehouses full of unread books; and 2) more importantly, no one could articulate his vision the way he could. The fact that he had no experience in education only meant that he needed to enlist a co-author with expertise in education.

He heeded my advice and went on to write the groundbreaking book *Disrupting Class: How Disruptive Innovation Will Change the Way the World Learns.* He wrote the book with Curtis Johnson, an education expert, and Michael Horn, Clay's Harvard graduate school student who did all the heavy lifting. Michael Horn coined the term "blended learning" for a curriculum that introduced technology into K–12 education. The early agreed-upon definition of blended learning accepted by its proponents reads as follows below.

> The definition of blended learning is a formal education program in which a student learns:
>
> 1. At least in part through online learning, with some element of student control over time, place, path, and/or pace
> 2. At least in part in a supervised brick-and-mortar location away from home
> 3. The modalities along each student's learning path within a course or subject are connected to provide an integrated learning experience

Michael is also the co-author of *Choosing College*, *The Blended Workbook*, *Private Enterprise and Public Education*, and *Blended: Using Disruptive Innovation to Improve Schools*.

Michael and I developed a close relationship that endures to this day (he's young enough to be my grandson), and he gave me credit in the book's acknowledgments for my contributions. Michael is that rare combination of an extremely accomplished, smart person who is genuinely nice. Whenever I've reached out to him both professionally and personally, he has been there for me.

When I decided to retire at the end of 2020, I planned a retirement party in May to coincide with the annual meeting of the NewSchools Venture Fund, run by my old friend Stacey Childress. Because of the pandemic, I had to cancel the event. Michael stepped in and organized a virtual retirement "party" in November 2020 on Zoom. My colleagues, friends, and family attended, including Sal Khan, founder of Khan Academy, and the event brought together people from the two parts of my professional life: stalwart supporters of school choice and champions of blended, competency-based learning. Their comments warmed my heart and brought back such fond memories of my interactions with them over the years. My daughter had the biggest laugh line. She said that I measured the success of a conference by how good the opportunity to dance was. Michael then showed a video of me dancing at his wedding.

Speaking of dancing, I want to tell you about a funny experience I had at one of the NewSchools Venture Fund's annual meetings. The dinners always featured dancing. It's not unusual for me to be the first person to get up and dance, and this time I partnered with a good-looking man in his late forties. He gave me a run for my money and escorted me to a table to rest (I was in my late seventies at the time). When I went outside for a breath of air, someone asked me if I knew whom I was dancing with. I said I did not, but he was a terrific dancer. She told me excitedly that it was MC Hammer, and in my total ignorance of contemporary music, I confessed I didn't know who that was. This story made the rounds, and for a time a picture of me dancing with MC Hammer appeared on Stacey Childress's media platform. It's probably still wandering around in cyberspace.

Back to Clayton Christensen. He published *Disrupting Class* in 2008, and suddenly, what I had been preaching for three years gained the credibility of a distinguished, brilliant academic. This seminal book changed the national conversation about bringing education into the twenty-first century. Clay founded Innosight Institute, a think tank whose mission was to introduce disruptive innovation in education and in health care. The Hume Foundation was its first donor. I became a founding board member and for the next six years, biannually, I had the incredible privilege of literally watching a great mind at work. Unfortunately, Clay was plagued by many health challenges, so much so that he was the cover story in the February 2011 issue of *Forbes* magazine, entitled, "Clayton

Christensen: The Survivor." Because of his failing health, I took over as chair of the board of the institute for the last three years of my tenure.

During this time, I also served as a board member for several other nonprofits to which the Hume Foundation made grants, including the Center for Education Reform and the State Policy Network. Unlike my colleagues at big national foundations who were not allowed to serve on the boards of the nonprofits they funded, I was fortunate to work with these organizations. I had a say in their strategic decisions, and it only made me more effective in the investments the Hume Foundation made. I became a member of iNACOL (International Association for K-12 Online Learning), now named Aurora Institute, run by an incredibly dedicated and efficient woman, Susan Patrick. The organization's mission is "to drive the transformation of education systems and accelerate the advancement of breakthrough policies and practices to ensure high-quality learning for all."

By 2012, it was obvious that the movement started by *Disrupting Class* was gaining ground. However, given the vagaries of the public-school procurement system, the plethora of new products hitting the market, and the woeful lack of training, the need for a coordinator became evident. Much like other aspects of the K–12 education system, the public-school procurement system is labyrinthine with endless rules and regulations and rife with cronyism and corruption, as most governmental endeavors are.

By that time, the Hume Foundation had invested $550,000 in three start-up blended-learning charter schools: Rocketship Education, Carpe Diem, and KIPP Empower. Having secured a grant from the foundation's trustees for KIPP Empower principal Mike Kerr to open the K–4 school in August, it occurred to me that there was no existing turnkey model available.

I reached out to Michael Horn in a panic, and he contacted Anthony Kim, who was enjoying a vacation in Hawaii after having sold his education technology company, Provost, and retiring. Anthony had founded Provost to provide software and services to operate online schools, so he was the perfect person for the job. In four months, Anthony designed the pedagogical blended-learning model for KIPP Empower and went on to found successful companies that continue to provide districts with the expertise they need to implement blended learning. Anthony is also a Corwin Press bestselling author, whose books include *The New Team Habits, The New School Rules,* and *Personalized Learning Playbook.*

Those investments in the three blended-learning charter schools began in 2010, and by the 2011–2012 school year, other foundations—including the Gates Foundation and the Broad Foundation, two giants in the school-reform space—granted upward of $40 million to schools adopting blended learning. There is no question in the field that the pioneering work of the Hume Foundation, both in contributing to the content of *Disrupting Class* and making bets on early versions of blended-learning schools, had an immense impact on philanthropic activity in K–12 education.

In 2012, I met Joe Wolf. He had just retired in his early forties from his position as a partner at RS Investments, where he co-managed a team that grew $100 million in assets to over $15 billion. I was introduced to Joe by Jay Jacobs, the then head of the nonprofit Summer Search and Jerry Hume's son-in-law (connections at work again). Joe is passionate about education and very active in the social-impact sector, focusing on K–12 education. He is co-founder of Imagine, an education nonprofit focused on eradicating illiteracy across the globe. We discussed the K–12 landscape, and he suggested investigating the creation of an organization that could tackle the challenges of the burgeoning blended-learning industry. There was a critical need for some entity to bring order to the Wild West of integrating technology into K–12 education. Over lunch, we agreed that the Hume Foundation would hire consultant Scott Ellis to explore the scope of such an endeavor and the need for it.

We contracted for three months of Scott's time, but at the end of six weeks, he was ready to present his findings. Unsurprisingly, he confirmed the need for a framework to coordinate the many aspects of blended learning and to identify the barriers that stood in the way of bringing schools into the twenty-first century.

In the summer of 2012, I had a serendipitous meeting with Stacey Childress, the then head of the Gates Foundation's K–12 Next Generation Learning team. Stacey had served briefly as a board member of the Innosight Institute before she joined the Gates Foundation. We knew each other from that experience—further evidence that relationships and connections are everything. As I was standing on the lawn at a Stanford University cocktail party, with my heels sinking in the turf, the sun shining in my eyes, and my shoulder hurting from what would turn out to be a torn rotator cuff, we talked about the need for an ecosystem coordinator for the blended-learning industry. I explained that the Hume Foundation had hired Scott Ellis to survey the field and told her of his recommendations to create such an organization.

After the meeting, I sent Stacey an outline of what that organization would do and a proposal that Scott Ellis submitted. In November 2012, the newly launched Learning Accelerator received a $750,000 grant from the Gates Foundation. Based on that commitment and the credibility it gave to the project, the Hume Foundation trustees met with Joe Wolf and Scott Ellis to hear their pitch. When they left the conference room, Jerry and George proposed a $2 million grant—a large sum indeed, but I argued that this was our opportunity to truly advance blended education and that we could make an even more impactful investment. They agreed. We gave the Learning Accelerator a $5 million grant, which was by far the largest grant we had ever made. Normally we made grants in the $25,000 to $100,000 range that had to be renewed every year, so over time, some of our grantees received a total of $1 million, but the grant we made to the Learning Accelerator in 2013 was drawn down over two years.

In this new phase of my professional life, I also met and worked with a kindred soul, Sal Khan, the founder of Khan Academy. Like me, Sal has transformative ideas for education. He's an unassuming Silicon Valley person and founded a non-profit organization in 2006 that created online educational tools for anyone to use for free. Khan Academy produces short lessons in the form of videos about all kinds of topics and supplements them with exercises and additional materials for educators to use. The lessons have been translated into dozens of languages, and one hundred million people use the platform worldwide every year. Michael Horn introduced me to Sal in January 2012 when we visited a fifth-grade class in the Los Altos School District that was piloting Sal's math program. No orderly rows of desks in this classroom; kids worked in groups or alone, some of them sitting on the floor. It was thrilling to see the concept of personalized education in its first iteration outside of elite, small-class-size private schools or personal tutors. I had heard Sal speak about this model at so many conferences, some of which I was instrumental in arranging, that I felt I could give most of his presentation myself.

I can't leave this part of my life story without mentioning meeting my best friend, Marina Walne, at a Philanthropy Roundtable conference. Although she's not a household name,

Marina has accomplished so much in her life in the field of education that she should be. When I met her, she worked for the Arnold Foundation in her native state of Texas, and we intersected in our passion for blended learning. She was doing an incredible job identifying innovative investments, but unlike my situation where the trustees of the Hume Foundation trusted me and gave me an enormous amount of leeway, this was not her case at the Arnold Foundation. After fourteen months on the job, she left the Arnold Foundation and since then has been involved in several projects that benefit from her experience and wisdom. I recruited her to be a founding board member of the Learning Accelerator, which gave us the opportunity to meet on a regular basis for board meetings from 2013 to 2019. We both attended five SXSW EDU Conferences and spent quality time together at her pied-à-terre in Austin. She and her husband, Tracy, came to my eightieth birthday party, flying to San Francisco from Houston specifically for that event.

I also want to acknowledge Scott Ellis's contributions. He has continued to play a big role in my life. He introduced me to Sue Toigo, an amazing woman and the founder of the Robert Toigo Foundation, whose mission is to build stronger, more diverse organizations through the inclusion and advancement of underrepresented talent, and mentor those individuals as they take their place in the world of investment and finance. Sue has been extremely helpful as I worked on this autobiography; she was the first person outside of family members who read the opening chapters. She then facilitated my contacts with the professionals I needed. More than that, we are soul mates and I have made a friend for life. Once a month, courtesy of Zoom, we laugh and cry together.

CHAPTER 19

As I continued my work in blended learning, I participated in the executive committee of Digital Learning Now!, an organization founded in 2010 and co-chaired by former governor Jeb Bush and former governor Bob Wise. It brought together a distinguished group of one hundred advisors who, over one hundred days, developed a ten-point platform that outlined the Ten Elements of High-Quality Digital Learning and how state legislators and policy makers could implement them.

This exciting experience solidified my relationships with the two former governors and the respective organizations they headed, Jeb Bush's ExcelinEd and Bob Wise's Alliance for Excellent Education. That the blended-learning movement attracted two champions from both sides of the political spectrum is testimony to its ideological neutrality. The Hume Foundation had consistently funded both Bush's and Wise's foundations over a period of ten years, which gave me an entrée to their respective inner circles. Jeb Bush dubbed me "the first lady of the digital movement," and I introduced Jeb and Bob Wise at the Excellence in Action 2011 conference that launched the movement. Jeb gave me a shout-out at another event and told the audience that the initiative he was launching wouldn't happen fast enough for Gisèle Huff. I had become well known for both my sense of urgency and my depth of knowledge. Imagine my delight when, at a Philanthropy Roundtable conference, a survey asked the audience to rank their expertise in the field of blended learning as novice, intermediate, expert, or Gisèle. Good times.

Governor Bush had an executive director who ran his organization, while Governor Wise acted as the hands-on CEO of his. We worked on several projects together and had many productive conversations in my office on the twenty-eighth floor of the Transamerica building. Bob is an excellent listener, and I often came away from our meetings buoyed by his enthusiastic response to suggestions I made. I served on the advisory board for Harvard University's Program on Education Policy and Governance for several years and saw Jeb regularly at annual board meetings. I consider him a friend, and our relationship is a perfect example of how I can get along and work with people with whom I disagree about some things. As I became a proponent of blended learning, a position that Jeb also embraced, I left behind the school choice movement, but Jeb remained one of its most vocal proponents. This led to a number of animated conversations.

In 2013, the Convergence Center for Policy Resolution, an organization that brings together people with diverging viewpoints to tackle societal problems, contacted me. They wanted to create a project around the ever-present challenges in K–12 education and asked if I would be interested in participating. They aimed to bring together a disparate group of twenty-eight people, including charter school operators, district superintendents, public-school board members, foundation program officers, and representatives from both national teachers' unions, the National Education Association (NEA) and the American Federation of Teachers (AFT). Although I have never been a believer in the work of committees, because I find them time-consuming and not very effective (both at University High School and at the Hume Foundation, I ran a one-woman office), I couldn't help but notice that on the Convergence roster, there wasn't one person associated with the blended-learning movement or anything having to do specifically with the use of technology as an integral part of the curriculum. I decided to participate, if only to speak for a transformative idea in a group of people mired in the status quo.

The first meeting that I attended was a dud. To finalize the list of participants, we met in Convergence's Washington, DC, office. We spent most of the time going around the table making introductions, an exercise that is anathema to me. It means that people drone on for at least five minutes, identifying themselves and going on and on about the mission of their organization. In my view, this boring exercise serves no purpose. Ostensibly to break the ice and acquaint people with each other, these introductions usually devolve into self-serving monologues that achieve very little. Convergence wisely followed up this initial meeting with individual telephone conversations to determine who would participate in the project.

Having settled on the participants, Convergence planned to hold six meetings over a period of eighteen months that would lead to a written document yet to be defined. The first meeting, which I did not attend, was explosive. Two well-known adversaries—Randi Weingarten, president of the AFT, and Rick Hess, senior fellow and director of education policy studies at the American Enterprise Institute—went at it in such a way as to leave the project in doubt. Both Randi and Rick are very articulate and passionate proponents on opposite sides of the public education debate. Convergence had to regroup, and under the extraordinary leadership of Kelly Young, the second meeting was put in the hands of the amazing consultant Allan Cohen and an outstanding team of facilitators led by David Friedman.

Forgive what may sound like hyperbolic praise, but this group took a major challenge and transformed it into a collaborative work heavily cited to this day. These leaders first demanded that we leave the present behind and imagine that anything was possible. By letting go of our animosities and ideological agendas, we were able to imagine a future for K–12 education that would serve all of America's children.

Over the course of meeting for two and a half days every other month, breaking bread together, and sharing our life stories over a glass of wine, we came to respect and even like one another—no matter what side of the issue we were on. Our success gives credence to the saying that "change happens at the speed of trust." We came to trust each other enough to work in earnest on a shared vision. During this experience, I made a friend for life of Becky Pringle, the then vice president of the NEA, the very organization that was the bête noire of the first half of my career, given that one of the goals of the school choice movement was to disempower the teachers' unions.

At the beginning of the Convergence project, we asked ourselves the question seldom raised: "What is the purpose of education?" And to that question we gave a specific, twenty-first-century answer in our vision document: "To enable all children to fulfill their full potential as empowered individuals, constructive members of their communities, productive participants in the economy, and engaged citizens of the US and the world."

The Convergence vision document characterizes the previous worldview as that of the industrial age and the current worldview as the networked age of the twenty-first century. In the previous worldview, the main purpose of education was the transfer of knowledge from one generation to the next. In the twenty-first century, it's now possible to use Google to find out anything you want to know in a second, so the purpose of education must evolve. The mere transfer of knowledge in the information age is necessary but no longer sufficient. We need to impart to our children the skills and dispositions they need to navigate the technological marvels we enjoy today and those in the future that we cannot even envision.

In the vision document, to ensure development in knowledge, skills, and dispositions for all learners, the group envisioned learning experiences characterized by the following five interrelated elements. Taken together, they formed the new, transformational design for learning:

- Learner Agency
- Socially Embedded
- Personalized, Relevant & Contextualized
- Open-Walled
- Competency-Based

The vision document proved to be a North Star for how to prepare children for the new age and how to equip students to confront its challenges. Given the recent dizzying pace of change in the world, we could not have predicted what our children would face today, and it's clear that we're still not providing them with tools to succeed in the future. You can read the vision document here: https://education-reimagined.org/wp-content/uploads/2021/01/A-Transformational-Vision-for-Education-in-the-US.pdf. It's eleven pages long, and the twelfth page lists the twenty-eight people from disparate backgrounds who created it.

Our success led to the creation of a stand-alone, spin-off nonprofit, Education Reimagined, led by Kelly Young. It was founded in 2014 to promulgate the vision document and guide others in establishing learner-centered environments. More than half of the signatories of the vision document continued to meet as its advisory board. In that role, we helped launch Education Reimagined and promoted the message in our networks and at education conferences. Kelly is an amazing leader, and she and I had many discussions about the activities of the organization and developed a close friendship.

I can't stress enough the importance of overcoming ideological barriers to reach a shared goal. One instance stands out to me as an excellent example of the power of collaboration. At the 2015 annual conference of ExcelinEd held in Washington, DC, Jeb Bush agreed to let me invite Becky Pringle, and I had the pleasure of seeing him, the champion of school choice, and Becky, the vice president of the teachers' union, civilly and cordially breaking bread together. To this day, Becky (who is now president of the NEA) and I do a dog and pony show about how far apart we were and how close we are now after setting aside our differences and focusing on our mutual love of children and our shared vision of improving education.

I'll forever be proud of my work on blended education. I've received many honors, one of the most memorable being at the 2015 iNACOL Blended and Online Learning Symposium. I appeared on a panel with Becky, moderated by Kelly Young, the executive director of Education Reimagined. It was Veterans Day, November 11, 2015, and there were over three thousand people in the audience, enthusiastically listening to our vision of the transformation of learning. After we answered Kelly's last question, she invited the chair of the board of iNACOL, Mickey Revenaugh, to come to the stage. I was nonplussed about this development, but since it was the last keynote session of the symposium, I expected closing remarks from Mickey. However, when she began speaking, I couldn't believe my ears. She announced that the board had decided to create the Huff Lifetime Achievement Award, of which I was the first recipient! I was bowled over as I listened to her. I couldn't believe that my fellow board members had pulled this off without my getting a whiff of it.

The award itself is a beautiful statuette, which Mickey said would only be given from time to time to recognize outstanding contributions to the work we're doing. This moment was the peak of my career and coincidentally marked the seventeenth anniversary of my joining the Jaquelin Hume Foundation. As I rose to accept the honor, I could think only of sharing with the audience my background, and how I made my life in the United States. I was sure to make the point on this Veterans Day that without the American army rescuing me from the horrors of World War II, I would not be standing here. "I am the embodiment of the American Dream," I said, and I mentioned how my late mother's encouraging words spurred me on to success. She said that I talked so well, I could convince anybody of anything. I ended my comments by raising the statuette and exclaiming, "Mom, I did it!"

Part III

CHAPTER 20

My passion for empowering children to understand *why* they are learning and *how* they are learning, rather than merely *what* they are learning, dovetailed with an issue my son, Gerald, was passionate about. At the time, he was a principal software engineer at Tesla and led the team that worked on the Model 3. He was very concerned about the challenges we'd face as we lose jobs due to technological advances. Although technology has provided countless improvements to our lives, he worried that those improvements would redound to the same small group of people who always have been in power and would leave the rest behind. He also foresaw a devastating time of transition between the time automation replaced human labor and the time our institutions could adjust to an entirely new definition of work. For that reason, he became a passionate proponent of universal basic income to ensure that, during the Fourth Industrial Revolution, every adult had a financial floor to support them in the form of a direct monthly cash payment with no strings attached. As the economy collapsed into the Great Recession, he set about to convert me.

In 2008 I was deeply steeped in the Libertarian worldview. When I ran for Congress in 1996 to 1998, then representative Tom Campbell of California endorsed me and introduced me to some members of the Republican caucus in Congress on a visit to Washington, DC. He portrayed me as a fan of Ayn Rand, which I was, ranking personal responsibility and persistence as the virtues that had led to my success thus far. For me, personal achievement was the motivating factor of my life, be it getting a PhD after starting college at the age of thirty-two or deciding to run for Congress with no previous experience and no connections to politics. I expected that personal achievement should motivate other people as well. It is the accumulation of the striving of individuals, I believed, that advances our civilization.

The Great Recession of 2008 to 2009 was a wake-up call for me. I realized that the millions of people who lost their jobs, their homes, and their way of life were not at fault. In my mind's eye, I pictured a fifty-two-year-old man being downsized—a man who had worked for thirty years in middle management, earning a $75,000 salary, dutifully paying his taxes, his mortgage, and his bills. What employment options did he have in this economy? Greeter at Walmart? Flipping burgers? No one was hiring. He could go back to school. But for what? The system had betrayed this man, and all the other men and women like him. He had no control over the system. He had been manipulated by those hungry to increase their profits in the most reckless manner. This man and all the people adversely affected by the recession should not be blamed for the criminal behavior of those in charge of the economic system.

As usual, those hit especially hard were marginalized people living in inner cities and dying rural areas. The burgeoning gig economy did little to help because job insecurity was built into the very structure of that work. As I often argued when advocating for K–12 education reform, you can't give people responsibility without giving them control.

Although I was not affected personally, I had never witnessed such a far-reaching economic catastrophe in America. I had lived through economic downturns brought on by the energy crunch, stagflation, and the dot-com bubble, but nothing was as far reaching or as blatantly unfair as the devastation of the Great Recession. This realization began to chip away at my Libertarian belief in the free market.

It became clear to me that mature capitalism, following the era of greed in the 1970s to 1980s, had abandoned reinvesting in the future. I had to reconsider my belief that capitalists are job creators who regulate supply and demand and keep economies in equilibrium. In 1776, Adam Smith wrote in *The Wealth of Nations* that "Consumption is the sole end and purpose of all production; and the interest of the producer ought to be attended to only so far as it may be necessary for promoting that of the consumer." With the advent of credit cards in the 1950s, the economy began to fall out of equilibrium. Consumers could easily purchase goods and postpone payment. Advertising agencies became more and more sophisticated and created ads that enticed consumers to buy what they thought they wanted, rather than what they needed. The accumulated credit card debt in America today is a staggering $806 billion. And let's not forget the student debt, which is an astounding $1.56 trillion.

Meanwhile, American families can no longer survive on one salary. I grew up, married, and had children in an America where most middle-class families who did not face race barriers could afford to buy a house, own a car, and take vacations. Income inequality was much less of a problem than it is now. In his book *Coming Apart*, published in 2012, Charles Murray describes how America changed between 1960 and 2010. He argues that people are prisoners of their zip codes and no longer mingle outside of their class. In the book he shows that in the twenty-first century, most people stick with those they know, and they take part in activities that occur in the neighborhood where they live. The rich associate with the rich and the poor associate with the poor, resulting in a lack of understanding and empathy, which has led to resentment and the deterioration of our social fabric. We can see this phenomenon playing out today, after the election of Donald Trump in 2016, which deepened the political divide. While his supporters waited for him to become "more presidential," he destroyed not only the presidency but the fundamental belief in voting as a legitimate and sacrosanct expression of the will of "We the People." But I will not spend any more time on the former president. Much has been written and continues to be written about him and how his administration tore apart the fabric of American society. I have nothing of value to add, and I don't want to spend more time venting about the many outrages he perpetuated and continues to perpetuate. I must let go.

Universal basic income could effectively narrow the wealth gap and class divisions. The idea of UBI has been around for centuries, going back to Thomas Paine and embraced by many great minds. In modern times, conservative economist Milton Friedman and social justice icon Martin Luther King Jr. were proponents of a guaranteed cash transfer to provide economic security for all Americans.

In his seminal book *Capitalism and Freedom,* Friedman wrote:

> We should replace the ragbag of specific welfare programs with a single comprehensive program of income supplements in cash—a negative income tax. It would provide an

> assured minimum to all persons in need, regardless of the reasons for their need. . . . A negative income tax provides comprehensive reform which would do more efficiently and humanely what our present welfare system does so inefficiently and inhumanely.

In his last book, *Where Do We Go from Here: Chaos or Community?*, Martin Luther King Jr. wrote, "I am now convinced that the simplest approach will prove to be the most effective—the solution to poverty is to abolish it directly by a now widely discussed measure: the guaranteed income." He went on to write:

> We have come to the point where we must make the nonproducer a consumer or we will find ourselves drowning in a sea of consumer goods. We have so energetically mastered production that we now must give attention to distribution. Though there have been increases in purchasing power, they have lagged behind increases in production. Those at the lowest economic level, the poor white and Negro, the aged and chronically ill, are traditionally unorganized and therefore have little ability to force the necessary growth in their income. They stagnate or become even poorer in relation to the larger society. The problem indicates that our emphasis must be twofold. We must create full employment, or we must create incomes. People must be made consumers by one method or the other. Once they are placed in this position, we need to be

> concerned that the potential of the individual is not wasted. New forms of work that enhance the social good will have to be devised for those for whom traditional jobs are not available.

Here Reverend King echoes Adam Smith's admonition that consumption is more important to the economy than production and foreshadows the rise of automation and the changing nature of work in the twenty-first century. Of course, embracing this concept requires a mind shift. We must leave our prejudices behind, as well as all the baggage that we have accumulated since President Reagan's diatribe about welfare queens and the failed theory of trickle-down economics. It is not true that a high tide raises all boats; it depends on whether you're on a yacht or a leaky canoe. Just as those wiped out by the Great Recession were not at fault, the poor in our society today are not at fault. It is very hard work to be poor. For those who depend on social welfare programs, it's a full-time job to jump through the bureaucratic hoops.

The working poor often juggle multiple jobs and endure inhumane and exploitative working conditions. They live from paycheck to paycheck, and 40 percent of the American people would have difficulty meeting an unexpected $400 expense, with 19 percent literally unable to do so. It's frightening to imagine being in this position. If your car breaks down, or you're charged with a misdemeanor but can't make bail, or your childcare arrangement changes, your whole life could go into a downward spiral. You could lose your job, your housing, and eventually, your family, for want of $400.

I am deliberately using the second-person possessive pronoun because the mind shift requires us to walk in these people's shoes. Imagine if that was your life. How would you handle such a situation? And don't tell me you would go out and get a good-paying job, because if you're adequately educated and you're white, no matter what your family circumstances are or what obstacles you had to overcome, you had a leg up. Most of the working poor are from communities that have been marginalized for generations. Just think of the yawning chasm that exists between the members of the Daughters of the American Revolution and the descendants of the Black slaves who lived alongside them.

Many of those who struggle to keep their heads above water are essential workers. As we all witnessed, the COVID-19 pandemic dramatically revealed the interconnectedness of our society. We owe so much to the essential workers. Those of us who had the luxury of working from home and retaining our paychecks would not have survived without the food processors, the truck drivers, the grocery clerks, the delivery drivers, and most of all, the entire medical profession. Most of these essential workers earn shamefully low wages. That is the crux of the matter. In the most prosperous nation in the history of the world, doesn't every human being deserve to live a decent life? Mature capitalism ignores the fact that the world is awash with capital—it is no longer as scarce as it was at the beginning of the first Industrial Revolution. The twenty-first century must address the problem of the distribution of wealth. How do we sustain an economy when the people who are its backbone cannot even afford decent housing?

During the pandemic the economic divide only deepened: more billionaires were created, existing billionaires got richer, and the stock market soared. Here are some staggering statistics: In America, the top 10 percent of wage earners average more than nine times as much income as the bottom 90 percent. But more astounding is that the nation's top 0.1 percent earn over 196 times the income of the bottom 90 percent. There is no moral, philosophical, or economic rationale for this inequity. The plutocratic nature of our government and its influence on the political class have overwhelmed the will and the needs of the people. The accumulation of money for its own sake is pointless. A billionaire can never spend all his money because while he sleeps, his wealth continues to accrue without his having to do anything. Hard work did not create today's billionaire class. They benefited from the peculiar institutions of hedge funds and investment banking, which led to the Great Recession. Mind you, these institutions are supposedly regulated by governmental agencies like the Securities and Exchange Commission, but those agencies were co-opted either unknowingly or deliberately, and they closed their eyes to the abuse of power.

Human nature is such that wants are infinite, so that a person who accumulates $1 billion, more than they could ever spend in their lifetime or those of their heirs, strives to add another billion. We are living in the Age of Scarcity, whose premise is that competition propels the innovations that improve the human condition and is based on the concept of a zero-sum game.

Historically, as nomads and cave dwellers, we had little reason for conflict because resources were there for the taking. But when agriculture took hold some ten thousand years ago and survival was no longer a daily struggle, it gave rise to towns, cities, and eventually entire civilizations. Once humans had territory and possessions to accumulate and defend, competition became more prevalent and tapped into the dark side of human nature, leading to wars, unnecessary famines, and the oppression of most of humankind. Conversely, these events could not have happened if people didn't work together. This is not to say that I don't recognize and appreciate the achievements of civilization. It's just that I agree with Rutger Bregman, who wrote *Humankind: A Hopeful History*, in which he successfully argues that human beings are wired to collaborate, but the systems they've created lead them in the opposite direction.

To give an example of the difference basic income can make, I want to introduce you to Kevin Dublin, a poet and author of *How to Fall in Love in San Diego.* Kevin receives $500 a month basic income through the Guaranteed Income Pilot for Artists run by the Yerba Buena Center for the Arts in San Francisco. Here in his own words is how it has affected his life:

> What kind of impact could such a small amount of money have on such a limited amount of people over a short amount of time? And one answer is that it's the difference between catching up on rent and stressing over eviction after you lose income; it's the difference between a four year old's desire to live with his father still going on unfulfilled eight years later and it finally being fulfilled; it's the difference between being able to afford a cross country trip, connecting with family one hasn't seen in years, hearing the story of a father selling the shoes from his feet and jacket from his back to feed his two younger brothers when his mother was sick and never learning you have two great uncles who were lynched in trees you would pass on the road to the church you went to as a kid. But those are only from my own personal experiences as a participant in one of these pilots.

Kevin is just one of millions of people whose lives would vastly improve with basic income. Wrap your head around this: The minimum wage in the United States has been $7.25 an hour since 2009. The average hourly wage worker currently earns $18.78 an hour, but to stay within the recommended limit of spending no more than 30 percent of their salary on housing, that worker would have to earn $24.90 an hour to afford to rent a two-bedroom home and $20.40 per hour to rent a one-bedroom. In 93 percent of US counties, full-time minimum-wage workers can't afford a modest one-bedroom rental. Meanwhile, the Supreme Court just struck down a moratorium on evictions imposed because of the pandemic, ruling that it exceeded the Centers for Disease Control and Prevention's authority to impose it. At the same time, the Emergency Rental Assistance Program, which was included in two of the stimulus packages passed by Congress and allocated $46.5 billion, has distributed only 11 percent of the funds.

Part of the problem is that federal funds are funneled through the states, and many states are either incompetent or unwilling to ensure that funds reach those desperately in need. On paper these people are protected, but in real life oftentimes the cash doesn't reach them in time to prevent the risk of becoming homeless. The power of universal basic income is that it's distributed regularly, automatically, and unconditionally, with no strings attached. It is the only transitional solution to the unmet challenges of the twenty-first century. One of Gerald's contentions is that the rules we live under were written by men (nary a woman to be found at the July 1944 Bretton Woods Conference, where forty-four countries met to write new rules for the international monetary system) and can be rewritten by people. These rules are not set in stone.

I want to elaborate on the role of women and how little opportunity we've had to contribute to the *his*tory of *man*kind. It's no accident that our vocabulary reflects the reality of women's position in society. We've been sidelined for millennia and although we've made strides toward equality, we have not reached it. We have yet to succeed in protecting women against the predatory behavior of men in power. The physical abuse of women continues, as do political endeavors to control our bodies in ways not applicable to men, thereby flying in the face of the Fourteenth Amendment to the US Constitution.

At a more pragmatic level, we continue to fight for equal pay for equal work. It's our natural tendency to favor those who are "like me." Because most hiring and promoting decisions are made by men, women have more difficulty finding equal footing. Further complicating matters is the undeniable fact that women must take time off for childbearing and are more likely to be the primary caregiver—the parent who must look after sick children—which requires them to miss more work. Finally, many women are not as comfortable as men when asking for their due. My daughter, Michèle, wrote a wonderful book, *The Transformative Negotiator*, which addresses this problem and equips women and men alike with the tools to improve their interactions with others.

Income and wealth inequality will become even more extreme with the inevitable advancement of artificial intelligence (AI), which will continue to have a profound effect on the nature of work. As Gerald and I discussed many times, the Fourth Industrial Revolution is unlike the previous three revolutions, which were based on tangible things like coal, gas, nuclear energy, and computers. The Fourth Industrial Revolution is fueled by the manipulation of data and new technologies that use robotics to produce things. Technological unemployment is inevitable, and it is imperative that we counter its deleterious effects by providing an unconditional income floor to every individual.

Since the first Industrial Revolution, workers have sold their labor to those who had the capital to produce more and more goods at cheaper and cheaper prices. Workers continually fought for better working conditions and wages and in many cases succeeded in protecting their rights, enacting laws that are still in place today. What Gerald called the "Labor Content Fallacy," which is discussed in the next chapter, is that there is no situation that inexorably posits *human* labor to be the determinant. In other words, labor is always necessary for production, but it need not be human beings that provide it; robots can take their place. In the previous three revolutions, machines replaced the most arduous and inefficient human labor and led to an explosion of widely available goods. Most skeptics of technological unemployment overlook the fact that, with AI, it isn't physical labor or thinking that is being replaced; it is the actual functions of workers, both blue- and white-collar. Technology has displaced millions of employees at retailers and call centers, and overtaken large portions of work that lawyers, accountants, insurance brokers, and travel agents provide.

Of course, robots don't pay taxes or act as consumers, so to sustain the economy, the circulation of money has to be restructured. With universal basic income, some portion of the profits generated by production would be distributed equally to everyone to provide them with a baseline. There would still be room for entrepreneurs and innovators to earn more for their contributions, but the wealth gap would not be nearly as obscene as it is now.

CHAPTER 21

Here, I must give you a caveat. This chapter is written to give you a clear understanding of UBI and is heavy on the academics. If you bear with me, though, you'll astound your friends with your knowledge of a trendy topic that just happens to be the last, best hope for the human species.

At the heart of universal basic income are two concepts that have become more and more salient as technological advances have transformed the twenty-first century. The first posits that if the exponential growth of artificial intelligence continues, it will likely lead to an Age of Abundance as opposed to the Age of Scarcity in which we have been living since we left the caves. However, moving to an Age of Abundance depends on how we manage and distribute the benefits of technology. If done right, we could live in a world where everyone has enough water to drink, enough food to eat, and a roof to shelter under. We currently live in a world where middle-class citizens of wealthy countries maintain lifestyles that medieval kings would envy, especially when it comes to life expectancy and everyday comforts. But in poor countries and among poor people in wealthy countries, life continues to be very difficult.

To move to an Age of Abundance, we need to imagine a future where the cost of goods decreases drastically and production requires fewer resources. Do you remember when calculators first hit the marketplace? They were very expensive and considered quite the status symbol. After a few years, though, they became so widely available and cheap that banks gave them away when you opened an account. Now, they're completely out of circulation, no longer necessary because our phones feature a calculator function. These ubiquitous gadgets, hardly bigger than a pack of cigarettes, provide not just calculator capabilities, but access to the world's compendium of knowledge through the internet. Our phones have made calculators and even computers obsolete. They are magnitudes cheaper than IBM's mainframes and magnitudes more powerful.

Coupled with a decrease in consumerism among the younger generations and the push to distribute wealth more equitably, moving to an Age of Abundance will have a transformational impact on societies. Just think about what will happen with the advent of self-driving cars. It won't be necessary for anyone to own, maintain, and insure a personal car. For baby boomers, getting a driver's license and owning a car was a point of pride, a coming of age. It's completely different for Gen Z'ers (those born after 2000), where 40 percent of nineteen-year-olds do not have a driver's license thanks to the convenience of Uber and Lyft in urban environments and due to Gen Z'ers' concern about the environmental impacts of driving.

This is a powerful shift in our culture. In my parents' generation, middle-class men traded in their cars every two years just for the status it bestowed upon them. The size of cars increased as manufacturers catered to macho sensibilities, resulting in enormous gas-guzzling monsters. In October 1957, Toyota entered the US market and over time forced Detroit to change its ways. Additionally, in my generation, it wasn't so much the kind of cars we drove but how we drove them that led to increasing vehicular deaths and accidents. Here we can witness another mind shift thanks to the efforts of one bereaved mother who founded Mothers Against Drunk Driving (MADD). Because of her efforts, more stringent laws were passed, and now none of my contemporaries would dream of driving drunk, which we routinely did when we were young. Instead, we simply call Uber or Lyft.

I'm encouraged to see that younger people are much more concerned about work–life balance and are generally more interested in experiences than in accumulating things. Although they love their gadgets (I will never understand why they stand in lines around the block to be the first ones to buy the newest version of the Apple iPhone), they're concerned about the quality of their lives and often pressure their employers, especially the big tech companies, to take ideological positions that align with their own values. (Of course, this doesn't apply to low-wage workers who must devote all their energy just to stay afloat.) For someone who came of age in a generation preoccupied with status symbols, this is a big shift indeed.

The younger generation proves that societal mind shifts do occur, and that brings us to the second concept underlying universal basic income: the nature of work. Up until the twenty-first century, work was humans' raison d'être. Without work, we would not have survived. Interestingly, anthropologists have found that our cavemen ancestors actually "worked" about fifteen hours a week, and that was sufficient to ensure their survival—with a little time left over to decorate their caves with paintings. John Maynard Keynes, a world-renowned

British economist in the first half of the twentieth century, predicted that we would achieve a fifteen-hour week by the beginning of this century.

In the Age of Scarcity, fear of not getting our basic needs met fuels our incentive to work. I can't count the number of times I've been countered with "the dignity of work." But where is the dignity in the long hours required to "get ahead," the stress, the forgoing of family life, the endless commutes, the mindless meetings, and on and on. It's true that a good number of people, especially in developed countries, enjoy their work, but for billions of our fellow human beings, work is stressful, and depending on the industry, sometimes dangerous.

It doesn't have to be this way. Things can and should change. During the Industrial Revolution, children went to factories rather than school. People worked twelve hours a day or more in very hazardous conditions, and there was no recourse for the abuse and oppression perpetuated by employers. Eventually, laws were passed that provided more protection to workers. It took time to enact those laws, but these very same laws led to today's more civilized workplaces. Nevertheless, we have much more to do to ensure equitable distribution of work and income. Most importantly, we need to consider the contributions we all make beyond market value. For instance, care workers are notoriously underpaid or not paid at all, and without them (and other overlooked essential workers that saw us through the pandemic), our economy would collapse.

This reexamination of the definition of work is only one side of the UBI coin. The other side is the replacement of human labor by robots doing routine tasks better and faster than humans. A great number of tasks in both blue-collar and white-collar jobs are repetitious, which is exactly where robots excel. Think about it, when was the last time you went to a library for research or used a travel agent to plan a trip? How many times have you been frustrated by the lack of a human being at the other end of your troubleshooting phone call? How often do you use the automatic checkout at your grocery or drugstore?

Remember, the whole concept of a "job" stems from the eighteenth-century Industrial Revolution when people began to leave their homes, go to places like mines and factories, work a set number of hours doing repetitive, tedious tasks, got paid the least that the market would bear, and then went home. These people sold their labor in a system that considered them cogs in the economic machine. To put this in perspective, I'm going to treat you to an article that Gerald wrote for Medium that captures exactly why this revolution is different. I can't do better than to quote it in its entirety; it's a five-minute read:

> Those who argue against the risk of technological unemployment due to the coming wave of robotics, AI, and other disruptive technologies often point to what is known as the Luddite or Lump of Labor Fallacy. Their reasoning is as follows: "You Luddites believe that there is a fixed amount of labor to be done in any given economy at any point in time. When technology substitutes for labor in some industry, you think all of the displaced people must therefore become unemployed. But the reality is that when costs are lowered in that industry due to increased productivity, the savings are passed onto consumers, who spend those savings in other business sectors, which create jobs to meet the demand. Human desires are infinite, so there will always be new demand creating new jobs as automation lowers costs.

Of course, there is disruption, and displaced employees will need to retrain for the new jobs, but it has always worked out this way and always will."

Historically, this has, in fact, always been true. Outside of agriculture and large-scale manufacturing, each incremental unit of a good or service (especially a service) has required significant incremental human labor. The amount of labor varies by product or service, but until very recently there was essentially *nothing you could buy* that would not require additional human labor hours, either in its production, distribution, sale, or delivery.

We are at the very beginning stages, however, of a new era. Those who argue the Lump of Labor Fallacy are becoming guilty of a different kind of fallacy, the *Labor Content Fallacy*. There is no law of economics that states that producing a good or service *must* require human labor. It's just been that way so far because machines were incapable of performing the most basic of human tasks—communicating in natural language, sensing emotions, moving and operating in unstructured environments, processing information and making decisions, and manipulating wide varieties of objects large and small. Every business that wanted to innovate and deliver a valuable service or product *had to hire humans*, because there was simply no alternative.

In this new era, we can already see that machines and AI are steadily gaining these skills. IBM's Watson, Google's driverless car, Microsoft's real-time translation, Narrative Science's Quill, Cynthia Breazeal's Jibo, Rethink Robotics' Baxter and Sawyer, and DARPA's Atlas are the initial versions of systems that have the potential to replace people in jobs that were historically safe from automation. Over the next few decades, as new disruptive businesses emerge employing these technologies, they will provide goods and services with minimal human labor content. The historical connection between consumption and job creation will be broken.

This phenomenon is most obvious with digital goods, which exhibit essentially zero marginal cost of production. Imagine 100 million consumers who save money due to automation in some industry buying 100 million downloads of Taylor Swift's latest hit. How many new jobs are created by that $100 million of spending? Basically, zero. What if those 100 million people paid a dollar for a year of the WhatsApp messaging service? How many new employees would WhatsApp need to hire? Since they handled 450 million customers with a staff of less than 50, the answer is—not many.

This is a remarkable new development. Most businesses throughout history have had labor as their largest single cost and their front-line employee costs scaled with their number of customers. Of course, there are service businesses today where this remains true. If the 100 million people all decided to get more frequent haircuts, there is no doubt we would need a lot more stylists. The critical question is this: what direction do we think our economy and technology are headed? As more and more of our products and services are digitized and machines can handle more and more of once human-only tasks, I believe we are headed into a new kind of economy with vastly reduced labor content and therefore, far fewer jobs.

Some might argue that digital goods are too obvious an example of zero marginal labor content. What about physical goods? We will continue to crave physical objects after all, not just songs and movies and games that can be downloaded. So, let's project Amazon ten years from now, just based on the initiatives they have already undertaken. Our 100 million consumers take their savings and buy products online thru Amazon, no salesperson involved. The products themselves are made at highly automated facilities with very low marginal labor content. In ten years, Amazon warehouses will be completely automated. They are already testing prototypes of robots to replace the human "pickers" who stand for hours as a parade of Kiva robots bring shelving units to them, and a computer points a laser at the item they should retrieve. Customer orders will be loaded into self-driving trucks that navigate their way into neighborhoods, where drones or ambulatory robots complete the deliveries. The trucks, drones and robots will of course themselves be built in highly automated factories. Increased demand from consumers, increased economic activity, no increase in jobs for humans.

Of course, if you extend the timeline out further, that entire process could be disrupted by future generations of 3D printing. Drop a glass on the floor and shatter it? Talk to your smartphone for a few seconds and a new one will be printed within minutes. You pay for the design (unless it was open source) and $1 per pound for the raw feed stocks. That's it. No marginal human labor required.

What about the most labor-intensive sectors of the economy? In the US the highest growth in employment recently has been in food service, retail, education, and health care. With rising minimum wages, automation may very soon come to restaurants (Momentum Machines already has a self-contained burger making robot). Technology is poised to revolutionize education, with movements like micro-credentialing reducing the need for large faculties and administrations at big expensive institutions. Despite huge regulatory barriers, we are also starting to see innovations in health care, where within ten to twenty years we may very well be managing chronic diseases without the need for nurses and doctors.

Some will argue that the money flowing to these low or zero labor content businesses finds its way into the hands of the owners of capital or shareholders, who then invest it in new businesses—the so-called "job creators." But if their investments are in Facebook and WhatsApp, there are meager numbers of jobs created (despite many billions in returns). Even the unusual part-time employment offered to many by Uber is slated within decades to disappear as the Uber CEO has already indicated he prefers (and has begun investing in) fleets of self-driving cars.

People who discount the possibility of technological unemployment are guilty of believing the *Labor Content Fallacy.* We need to begin preparing for a different kind of economy. In an age of ubiquitous smart machines, we need to shift our mindset away from the goal of "full employment", as that will simply not be possible. While there will be infinite human wants and ever-expanding amounts of work to be done, we just won't need humans to do the work when machines can do it better and cheaper.

CHAPTER 22

As Gerald was introducing me to the concept of universal basic income, he was also searching for ways to widely promote the idea. One of his childhood friends happened to be connected to the Milken Institute, and in 2015, Gerald participated in a panel discussion at the Milken Institute Global Conference in Los Angeles. There he explained how unlikely it would be for the Fourth Industrial Revolution to create the number of jobs necessary to compensate for jobs lost to machines. He argued that training displaced workers for STEM (science, technology, engineering, and mathematics) jobs that the new economy would generate wouldn't be enough. At that time STEM jobs represented about only 9 percent of the economy, including about 1 percent for creative jobs in the arts and media. I attended that session as a guest, and I'll always remember how proud I was of Gerald at that moment.

His presentation was so well received (it ranked fourth in his time slot in an international conference chockfull of celebrities and pundits) that a speakers' talent company approached and hired him. His first gig was a presentation to a group of business executives in Zurich, Switzerland, in October 2015. The presentation earned him $45,000 and gave him the opportunity to meet up with my granddaughter, Jane, during her semester abroad. His topic was technological unemployment and how it would transform the world of work, requiring the implementation of UBI as a transitional solution. He organized and appeared at several other national conferences, part of his appeal being his position as a principal software engineer at iconic Tesla (although he never mentioned Tesla or anything to do with the company during his talks).

Gerald was also a member of Singularity University, founded by Peter Diamandis, a proponent of deliberately using technology to improve the quality of life. Gerald helped Peter organize a workshop that explored the challenges and opportunities of AI and technological unemployment. One of the participants was Martin Ford, bestselling author of the seminal book *Rise of the Robots: Technology and the Threat of a Jobless Future.*

Around this time, Gerald helped plan an event in Florida that included someone who personally knew Elon Musk, the CEO of Tesla. That person invited Elon to attend and mentioned that one of the presenters was a Tesla engineer. Gerald had received permission to participate in the event by someone at Tesla who, unbeknownst to him, was fired six weeks later. When Elon Musk heard that Gerald was a speaker, he called Gerald in personally and told him in no uncertain terms to cease and desist because he would not have the Tesla name bandied about. Even though Gerald had used the Tesla name only in his job title, and never mentioned the company in his presentations, Gerald complied and stopped making public appearances.

That did not, however, stifle his ardent interest in promoting universal basic income. By 2015, he had me completely convinced, and I made a $200,000 grant, in part funded by Jerry Hume, to Darrell M. West, the vice president and director of governance studies as well as a senior fellow of the Center for Technology Innovation at the Brookings Institution, to publish a paper on the topic. This was quite a departure for me. I had never made a contribution of that magnitude. In October 2015 Darrell published "What Happens if Robots Take the Jobs? The Impact of Emerging Technologies on Employment and Public Policy." The publication of the paper was followed by a conference at the institute in Washington, DC, where Nick Hanauer and Scott Santens argued the two sides of the question.

This was the first time I met Scott, someone whose belief in UBI was so deep that he devoted his career to researching and proselytizing it. He was subsidized by individuals who contributed to his Patreon account. Patreon is a website that enables patrons to support artists and researchers like Scott. It is yet another example of twenty-first-century collaboration in which people contribute with no expectation of returns on their investments. Other similar sites are Wikipedia, where people contribute time and knowledge, and GoFundMe, where people can contribute money to individuals, many of whom face dire circumstances often related to health-care costs.

Scott and Gerald worked together for more than a year. Gerald introduced Scott on national conference stages where he spoke about the merits of universal basic income. They edited each other's writings and spoke often, their great minds working together on the solutions UBI could provide in the face of technological unemployment. Scott is now a recognized and distinguished international expert on the topic.

Gerald was well aware that implementing universal basic income as a public policy would require a major mind shift. Because very few people even knew what universal basic income meant, he decided to make the concept accessible to the general public by writing a techno-thriller based on his deep knowledge of technology. He began writing in 2013, and it was a labor of love involving the whole family. He called upon his sister, Michèle; his daughter, Jane; and me to read and reread his manuscript. Given that his job at Tesla was very demanding, it took him five years to finish the book.

I'll come back to that in a bit, because first I want to reference Gerald's involvement with Andrew Yang, one of the 2020 candidates for the presidency of the United States. Gerald had read Andrew's book *The War on Normal People* in 2018 and became an early supporter of Andrew's campaign, as did I. The centerpiece of Andrew's stump speech was the endorsement of universal basic income as a first-step solution to technological unemployment. Like Gerald and me, Andrew feared that the lack of awareness of the changing world of work would be catastrophic. He worried about the lack of urgency and believed it imperative that the government prepare by implementing universal basic income immediately. Andrew anticipated that extreme upheavals would happen within ten to fifteen years and argued that provisions should be made without delay to meet the challenge.

Of course, his plea was ignored. Andrew was the only candidate who championed UBI. Because he generated a passionate following among mostly young people, he raised enough money, $41 million all told, to secure a spot on the debate stages of the Democratic presidential primaries. Although the moderators treated him shoddily and allocated the least amount of time to him despite his rankings, he took every opportunity to speak about universal basic income and his intention to provide every American over the age of eighteen with $1,000 a month, no strings attached.

Andrew's performance in the first debate made him realize

that, even though he was wildly popular on the campaign trail, he needed to improve his debate performance. He hired professionals to train him, and it so happened that he was in San Francisco for the first such session. I was enlisted to act as a stand-in for Senator Elizabeth Warren. For two hours I read from a script at a podium that replicated the primary debate stage—just one more unexpected and very meaningful experience for me.

I learned a great deal from my peripheral involvement in Andrew's campaign. One of the most important lessons I learned is that Twitter and other social media do not represent the voice of the people. Social media gives one a false sense of being part of a universe of people who think and feel the same way you do. But the reality of the electoral process is what happens in the voting booth. Andrew spent $10 million and deployed an army of volunteers who spent a full month knocking on doors in Iowa, but it gained him only 5 percent of the votes in the caucus.

Outside of his dedicated followers, universal basic income was a new concept for the majority of people. Most viewed it as an interesting topic but not a serious policy position that had any chance of being implemented. Although he dropped out of the race, much credit is due to Andrew Yang for putting UBI on the map. His efforts and the devastating effects of the COVID-19 pandemic have made UBI part of the national conversation.

To promote a wider understanding of the threat of technological unemployment and the need for universal basic income, Gerald set his book twenty years in the future. It depicts a dystopia of unrelenting and widespread surveillance, enhanced social media manipulations, and supercomputers. Because of his lifelong work in tech, Gerald had a deep understanding of what our future could look like. His book portrays a nation where the economy is ravaged by the takeover of robots, modern Luddites become terrorists, and technology is used to devastate society. The theme of Gerald's book is that technology can be incredibly good or incredibly bad, as his subtitle so aptly reflects: *Will Technology Ever Benefit Us All?*

His protagonist is a young Indian woman, Sarah, modeled after Malala Yousafzai, the Pakistani girl who was shot in the head by a Taliban gunman because she advocated for education rights for girls. Sarah becomes a spokesperson for a new worldview that places human beings at the center of economic systems. She starts holding conferences at universities and builds a huge following of young people who recognize that the future of the human species depends on the ideas that she is advocating for. She becomes a world-renowned messianic figure with a message that is particularly welcome in the chaos that technological unemployment has created in 2038.

Sarah spreads the message that technology is and always has been a force that has led to the incredible improvements in our modern society. Unfortunately, control of that technology, like control of societies over time, rests in the hands of the few, and instead of redounding to the benefit of everyone, technological advances lead to more and more immiseration. This gives rise to revolutionaries who want to stop technology in its tracks and do away with the institutions that support and promote it, including the government.

In the book a bipartisan group of six senators proposes implementing universal basic income. What Gerald describes is a foreshadowing of what we are experiencing now—a political establishment in gridlock. In Gerald's telling, the senators come to the table entrenched in their ideological frameworks and antagonistic toward each other. Based on the many conversations we had about my experience with Education Reimagined and how we arrived at consensus, Gerald conjured up a similar process in the book, which features a skilled facilitator and a demonstration by a TaskRabbit gig worker of what it means for a person to live in financial insecurity. It is a brilliant cautionary tale about what we're likely to face in less than two decades.

Andrew Yang contributed a blurb for the book, which reads, "*Crisis 2038* is a fascinating account of our near future. Only someone who is actively engaged in building the future like Gerald Huff could have crafted such a detailed look at what awaits us as a people and a society." And Scott Santens, a writer and full-time advocate of universal basic income, added, "This story takes place in a future United States that has not made the decisions it needed to make in the here and now. What transpires is an important warning by Gerald Huff of the kind of future we can realistically expect where due to political gridlock and corporate greed, technology continues to not be used for the benefit of all until the inevitable breaking point is reached . . . Is this the future we want, and what can we do to avoid it? Read it and find out."

Crisis 2038 has sold some 20,000 copies through Amazon and another 8,200 copies on SoundCloud, where it is available for free: https://fundforhumanity.org/book/. I strongly recommend that you read or listen to it. It's a page-turner.

CHAPTER 23

On Thursday, September 13, 2018, Gerald called to tell me that he had been experiencing acute pain in his stomach, which had woken him a couple of days in a row. I told him he must immediately go see his primary care physician, and he replied that he hadn't had a checkup since she had retired two years prior. After giving him the what-for, I insisted that he make an appointment, which he did on the following Monday. The doctor saw suspicious indications and ordered a biopsy. As it happened, I was the only member of the family (all of whom live in the East Bay except for me) who could drive Gerald to his 8:00 a.m. appointment.

I picked Gerald up and we chatted confidently about the procedure. We checked in to the hospital and he donned a hospital gown and climbed onto a gurney. I had a discussion with the doctor about what the procedure entailed. He told me that the suspicious area was around the pancreas but that he would perform the biopsy on the liver because it was more accessible. I asked him how the results would be accurate if they were not targeted, and he was surprised at the question, noting that I was a smart lady. He explained that whatever the biopsy showed in the liver would be the same for the pancreas. I gave Gerald a hug and left the room. I was beginning to feel apprehensive. After the procedure was over, I drove him home and he told me he would let me know as soon as the results came in. I went home in a daze.

On Friday morning, September 28, while I was home alone as usual, my daughter-in-law, Judy, called. She told me the biopsy showed that Gerald had pancreatic cancer. I let out a primal scream and slammed the phone down. I couldn't believe it was happening again.

As soon as she heard the news at her job at UC Berkeley, my daughter dashed to her car and drove to San Francisco to be with me. Between the time I hung up and the thirty minutes it took for her to get to my condo, I raged, screaming at the top of my lungs. She made me take deep breaths and eventually got me to stop screaming. She assured me that we would do everything possible to beat the cancer, but I knew in my heart and in my head that we couldn't. It was incomprehensible to me—I couldn't grasp the enormity of what was happening. I remember rocking myself in my chair, saying over and over, "My beautiful boy, my beautiful boy."

Just two weeks before, he had gone on a twenty-mile bike ride with Judy and was seemingly in good health. That weekend, Judy and Gerald had planned to go to Yosemite to celebrate their thirtieth wedding anniversary. Instead, his condition took a dramatic downturn, and he was admitted to the ICU at the Contra Costa Regional Medical Center in Martinez, where Judy works. When he was released, a period of frantic activity began.

Gerald's son, Paul, had stayed in Santa Barbara after he graduated from the University of California. He hadn't found himself and was working one inconsequential job after the other. When he learned about the diagnosis, he quit, packed up, and returned home. Our relationship was always somewhat strained for reasons I could never understand or explain, but when we first saw each other upon his return, he took me in his arms and said for the first time ever, "I love you."

Gerald's daughter, Jane, who had graduated from Northwestern University and worked in Los Angeles as a media editor, had just completed a gig and was between jobs. She returned home with all her media equipment and stayed until January. She became Gerald's assistant in putting the finishing touches on *Crisis 2038*, which became the focus of Gerald's waning energy as he was dying. She remains in charge of the book's distribution, and she and I speak on Zoom almost every week.

As soon as Gerald was released from the hospital, I reached out to my friend Bill Oberndorf for help. At the time, Bill was the chair of the board of UCSF, and he arranged for the world-class pancreatic cancer doctor on their staff, Dr. Andrew Ko, to examine Gerald and develop a treatment protocol. Dr. Ko established a regimen and Gerald began intensive chemotherapy administered at the hospital in Martinez. It had devastating effects on him. After the first treatment, his stomach swelled, his voice became shaky, and he lost his appetite. The doctors considered surgery, but ultimately determined that it was not feasible and scheduled a second round of chemotherapy. Gerald could still get dressed and sit up when he came home, but by then, we all knew he was terminal. He knew it, too, and in his typical fashion, he was very stoic. He never asked, "Why me?" and he never railed against the fates that had marked him for this disaster.

I tried to find the right level of involvement. Obviously, Judy was the primary person in charge of his care, and I didn't want to interfere with her decisions. I drove to Berkeley several days a week to be with Gerald. Before he entered hospice, we had frequent halting conversations, during one of which he held my hands and said, "Mom, this is déjà vu all over again for you." I replied, "Yes, but you know I'm a survivor." One time when we spoke over the phone, when I could barely make out his words, he said, "We have a special bond." And we did have a unique bond beyond that of a mother and son—we were intellectual soul mates.

All the while, Gerald was frantically putting the finishing touches on his novel. He was so consumed by the need to get it published properly that up until the day before he died, when he essentially could not speak anymore, had lost all his hair, and weighed half of his normal 210 pounds, he worked fervently on the book, making sure that everything, down to the infrequently used italics, was perfect.

I visited him on Thursday, November 15, when he was essentially comatose. My visit involved mostly rubbing his back and lying alongside him in bed. I kissed him goodbye and told him I would not be there the next day but would be back on Saturday. He murmured, "What day is this?" I told him it was Thursday, and in retrospect, it seems to me that he knew he wouldn't make it until Saturday. Those are the last words he spoke to me. When I returned on Saturday, November 17, he was in a coma from which he never awoke. He died that night, seven weeks after his diagnosis. I spent the day on one side of his bed and Judy sat on the other side, both of us holding his hands. I had begun to learn how to meditate at the onset of this nightmare, and I called on all my resources to survive the vigil.

Gerald was the most humane person I knew and always the smartest person in the room but completely egoless. As he said in the video Jane recorded on October 20, in which he addressed his future grandchildren, he liked people, but he didn't need people. He was not one for small talk, although he could hold his own when necessary. He was very self-aware and comfortable in his skin, passionate about things of interest to him and very capable in his pursuit of those things. He admitted in the video that he was not at all a networking person but pointed to the irony that all the jobs he had held were the result of connections he had made. He spent most of his career at Intuit and Tesla, with an antecedent stab at a start-up, Avantos, which lasted for six years but closed its doors because the online management product it developed was before its time.

People recognized how special he was. When he fell gravely ill, his colleagues at Tesla were shocked. A colleague delivered a pack of notes written to him, and I want to quote, with his permission, the words of his supervisor at Tesla, David Lau, because they capture not the impressions of a loving mother but those of someone who worked professionally with Gerald:

> Gerald, I don't know where to begin. It's still such a shock to even be writing this. You've been such a huge part of my experience at Tesla, and such an inspiration to me and the team. So often, I see your fingerprints on the way our products and systems work, and the way our teams operate, collaborate, and solve problems. I'm sure you know that you've built systems and software that have changed the world, but you should also know that the engineers you've mentored, the teams you've built, and the cultures you've shaped will continue to live in your image for a long, long time.
>
> You've been an invaluable partner, teacher, and coach to me, and I'm sure that's been true

> for every other engineer and leader you've worked with. I can confidently say that every time we've had a conversation, I've learned something, and walked away with a bunch of ideas about what I can and should do better, new ideas about what's possible and achievable, and in many cases, entirely new frameworks for thinking about problems.
>
> I wish dearly for all of us here to have the opportunity to work with you again really soon. I understand that a miracle would have to happen in order to make that come true. But while we hold out for that miracle, we'll channel all these things that you've taught us and given us, and keep you and your family in our thoughts.
>
> Thank you. I'm grateful for the time we've been able to spend together.

In the Greek tragedy of my life, I lost my husband at the age of fifty-four to pancreatic cancer, and thirty-one years later, I lost my only son to the same dreaded disease at the same age. Losing a child is an unspeakable disaster, and I use the word advisedly. People who lose their parents are orphans, and people who lose their mates are widows or widowers, but there is no word in the English language for people who lose a child. It's as if you have lost a piece of yourself because, in fact, you have—flesh of my flesh. The pain abates but never disappears, as it did for me after the death of my husband. When you lose your mate, it is possible to replace him with another person, but no one can replace the person you gave birth to.

Gerald's brother-in-law, John, and his wife, Kim, live in a beautiful historically designated house in the Oakland Hills with a sweeping view of San Francisco and the Bay. They are a power couple, very involved in politics and often hold fund- and friend-raisers in their home. They held a celebration of life for Gerald at their home on December 15, and 115 people gathered to participate. Family came from Los Angeles and friends came from as far as Florida, New York, and Louisiana. Fifteen of Gerald's Tesla colleagues attended, one of whom took the red-eye from New York and flew back the same afternoon. Kim is an accomplished hostess, and the event was beautiful and moving. The video that Gerald recorded in October ran on a loop in the family room, and everyone got a glimpse of who he was at a very personal level.

Michèle was the first person who spoke, and she was followed by Stephen Kuhn, Gerald's best friend. They met at University High School, shared a passion for computers, and remained friends through thick and thin. Stephen edited Gerald's book, toiling alongside him for five years, a role that Gerald recognized in the book's acknowledgments where he wrote, "My biggest thanks goes to my brother Stephen Kuhn, who provided not only detailed line edits for many drafts but also had an eagle's eye focus on character and plot inconsistencies." Other than close family members, Stephen was most devastated by his loss, and his eulogy was frequently interrupted by tears. Gerald and Stephen's former headmaster at University High School, Dennis Collins, also attended, as did Paul Chapman, who had been the dean of students, and Prudy Kohler, the school's art teacher, who taught Gerald how to drive a stick shift. Roy Goldman, who had worked with Gerald at Intuit and was instrumental in getting him the job at Tesla, described what an invaluable contributor Gerald was.

Scott Santens came from New Orleans to eulogize Gerald and spoke of Gerald's deep involvement in the challenges of technological unemployment and the transitional solution of universal basic income. I am extracting a portion of his eulogy here, where he called Gerald "a brother in mind" (emphasis is Scott's original).

> Gerald wanted to help lift humanity. That's why he supported the idea of basic income. It's literally **an investment in humanity** itself, where everyone starts with **something instead of nothing**, *unconditionally,* and is trusted to use it in their own best *and infinitely creative* ways.
>
> At first glance, the idea of everyone receiving a monthly cash dividend seems only about money, but that's only the vehicle of the meaning. It's a recognition that **everything that humanity has ever discovered, the fruits of the sum total of all our knowledge, to some degree belong to everyone, not just those at the end of a long chain that extends for millennia back to the very first tool.**
>
> Technology is a tool our species created, as is money. These tools can be wielded for our benefit or our downfall.
>
> Gerald knew that it's up to us to decide which.
>
> It's up to us to recognize that tools can cut on both sides, and that protections need to be engineered for optimal outcomes.
>
> It's up to us to make technology work for everyone, to reduce the fears of it and to expand its benefits to all, as our rightful human inheritance.
>
> Gerald knew that as long as tech doesn't

> lift everyone up, we'll pull against it, we'll slow its progress, and we'll be worse off instead of far better off.

Scott's eulogy beautifully captures Gerald's vision. I've dedicated the rest of my life to making his vision a reality.

CHAPTER 24

As you can probably surmise, I find it difficult to tolerate idleness. By the end of 2020, the Hume Foundation had spent down its corpus and the trustees decided to close its doors. Even as early as 2017 as I approached retirement, I worried about how I would fill my time. I explored various volunteer activities in San Francisco but didn't find a fit, and both Michèle and Gerald were concerned about my lack of direction. I had taken it in my head starting in 2015 that I wanted Michèle to move from Albuquerque back to the Bay Area to have her near me. Of course, I had no inkling that Gerald would fall ill, but if she had not been there, I don't know what I would have done.

Michèle was no longer happy at her job at the University of New Mexico. For three years, she assiduously pursued all leads but was stymied by ageism. The depersonalization of the job-seeking process, where algorithms eliminate excellent candidates because of some flag unrelated to what they have to offer, is to the detriment of the employers. She finally landed a very interesting job at UC Berkeley in September 2017. She is the director of the Office of Business Contracts and Brand

Protection and receives kudos from her subordinates and supervisors alike.

When she moved, her partner stayed behind in Albuquerque pending the sale of her house. Michèle moved in with Gerald and Judy and spent the next eight months at their home, where Terri joined her in December. In a very hot housing market, it took that much time to find an appropriate housing situation. For a while, we entertained the idea of buying a house together with an in-law apartment, but we couldn't find a setup as nice as my condo in San Francisco, so ultimately, we abandoned the idea. To this day, Michèle counts the time she spent with Gerald as a blessing.

In January 2019, I began to cast about in earnest for a solution that would sustain me for the rest of my life. Given my many years in the nonprofit world and my commitment to universal basic income, I decided to explore the possibility of starting an organization dedicated to building on the national conversation about UBI started by Andrew Yang's presidential campaign platform and all the work that Gerald had done himself. The rest of this book is aimed at fulfilling the mission statement of the organization I founded: "We work to raise awareness of universal basic income and to promote its understanding, acceptance, and implementation." I hope that you will appreciate what I aim to accomplish. Because I feel so strongly that mature capitalism has outlived its usefulness and technological unemployment looms for large portions of our population, I see this transitional solution as the only way forward.

After Gerald died, the family discussed what we could do to honor his memory. We talked about establishing a scholarship in his name, but we couldn't decide whom it would benefit or how it would be administered. That is how I came to create the Gerald Huff Fund for Humanity, a nonprofit 501(c)(3) organization that accepts tax-deductible donations. It's commonplace for high-net-worth individuals to start foundations that are exempt from taxation unless their investment revenue is more than $2 million per year. I'm not in that league, but over time and due to my frugal, conservative financial management, I've accumulated enough money to ensure my retirement, including a 401(k) to which I contributed for twenty-two years, matched by the Hume Foundation. I have only three heirs: my daughter and my grandchildren. They have other sources of long-term financial support, so I am not concerned about making them the exclusive beneficiaries of my holdings. So between my contribution and that of others (including a commitment by Susan and Bill Oberndorf to match my $100,000 for three years), I was able to raise $435,000 in 2019, more than enough to launch a nonprofit start-up without a payroll since I was its only unpaid employee. I intend to continue to fund it as long as I am physically and mentally able, with the help of my daughter-in-law, who shares my commitment to Gerald's vision. It gives me a powerful purpose at an age when such opportunities are rarely available. It also fulfills my lifelong need to be productive.

As for any other start-up and especially for a nonprofit whose activities have societal impact, I had to accomplish basic tasks: due diligence of the players and activities in the UBI field to ascertain what value I could offer, and creating a mission statement, a logo, and a launching strategy. I want to describe those to you because they represent a microcosm of any process of innovation and the basis for creating something out of nothing.

Most of the established UBI organizations were academic ones like Basic Income Earth Network, which was established in 1986 under the name Basic Income European Network (BIEN), or the North American Basic Income Guarantee

(NABIG), founded in 1999 as its American affiliate and which held its first conference in 2002. At gatherings of various sizes, scholars presented their research and respondents countered it as appropriate. Less prominent at these gatherings were the activists who promoted UBI on the ground.

Other than the remnants of the Yang Gang that continued their work after Andrew's withdrawal from the presidential race and his spin-off, Humanity Forward, whose mission was to distribute private donations in the form of UBI to individuals, there was only one other prominent organization in the field, the Economic Security Project (ESP). It was founded in 2016 with a grant from Chris Hughes, the original co-founder of Facebook with Mark Zuckerberg when they were both at Harvard. As a side note, when that organization was founded, Gerald was first on its list of contributors. ESP was and continues to be very prominent and active in the UBI space, having funded the Stockton pilot launched by then mayor Michael Tubbs in February 2019, which made a monthly $500 cash transfer to 125 randomly selected families for two years. This led to the creation of Mayors for a Guaranteed Income and almost one hundred other pilots currently being launched or planned all over the country. ESP lobbies for permanent cash transfers at the federal level. The co-founder and co-chair of the organization, Natalie Foster, has become a dear friend of mine. An ardent proponent of UBI, she has shepherded the movement through the legislative process of federal laws like the stimulus checks and the Child Tax Credit. She has boundless energy; a sunny, upbeat personality; and best of all, she gets things done.

Another partner in crime in the effort to make UBI a reality is Andy Stern, the former and now president emeritus of the Service Employees International Union, and a senior fellow at the Economic Security Project. He wrote a seminal book,

Raising the Floor: How a Universal Basic Income Can Renew Our Economy and Rebuild the American Dream. Together with Natalie, Andy and I speak on a regular basis to pool our resources and strategize how to continue the momentum of UBI. No great idea whose time has come can be translated into public policy by one person; it requires the commitment and collaboration of many people over an extended period.

It's interesting to note that, although prominent figures in the tech world such as Elon Musk, Richard Branson, and Mark Zuckerberg have paid lip service to UBI on many occasions, only Jack Dorsey, the founder of Twitter, and Chris Hughes have made considerable contributions to its promotion. Most UBI support has been channeled into pilots, which are important because proof of concept is an essential part of social change. But in my experience, pilots are not enough to change federal policy. You must organize a grassroots movement that will continually promote the policy.

My experience as a philanthropist had shown me that without infrastructure and without addressing systemic failures, project-based investments only go so far. In education, charter schools were the equivalent of UBI pilot programs, and as I detailed earlier, they turned out to be an incremental solution because replicating them was a Herculean task. UBI pilots are even more problematic because most are time-limited and do not use governmental dollars. Although investments are also being made into researching the benefits of the pilots, because the funds are temporary, they do not accurately indicate how a lifelong UBI program could benefit people. In any case, the costs of running a pilot are very high and exceeded my limited budget.

It was clear to me that there had been few attempts to deliberately change the hearts and minds of the American public. UBI communities had formed on social media, but they were composed of members of the same choir and mostly spoke only to each other. I decided that my organization, with its limited resources, would concentrate on public relations and ad campaigns to target the uninformed and unconvinced. I'm not sure if you fit into one of those two categories, dear reader, but if you do, I hope that I make you into a UBI proponent.

I also had to create and name the organization. Here again, my connections held me in good stead. Scott Ellis, the former CEO of the Learning Accelerator and current member of the board of the Gerald Huff Fund for Humanity, has an extensive network of talented people in different fields. As I was launching the fund, Scott introduced me to rick keating [*sic*], who heads an eponymous marketing and branding company. Rick took me on as a client even though most of his other clients are organizations with budgets orders of magnitude greater than mine. Because he believes in UBI, he took an interest in my project and we proceeded to first come up with the name, the Gerald Huff Fund for Humanity, and then line up all the domains in GoDaddy that ensured its integrity. These steps were entirely outside of my wheelhouse, and I would never have been able to do this on my own. Rick introduced me to many influential people and became a close friend. He is a man of integrity in a business that doesn't necessarily place a high value on that quality, and he cares deeply about UBI. I couldn't have found a better consigliere.

The fund needed a website, and rick recommended engageSimply, headed by a kindred spirit, Judy Shapiro. They designed the website as well as a news site, Basic Income Today (BIT), which tracks all things UBI on a daily basis. Scott Santens, a founding member of the board of the fund, also took on the job of editor of BIT. It is the go-to place for up-to-date UBI news not only in the United States but all over the world. It also covers the effects of technological unemployment.

BIT has created a community of people interested in UBI outside of the usual suspects. You can check it out here: https://basicincometoday.com/.

But engageSimply is much more than a vendor; they have become the fund's IT department, not only when it comes to maintenance and revisions, but when it comes to other endeavors such as applying for and obtaining from Google a $10,000 per month ad allowance and then creating and coordinating the ad campaigns. My éminence grise is Julien, who creates campaigns and whom I consider my alter ego. If only I could do what he does, I would do it the way he does it. We speak once a week to make decisions about ongoing projects and possible future projects. Julien is very good at thinking ahead and suggesting new ways to fulfill our joint mission.

The Gerald Huff Fund for Humanity is a family affair. My daughter is the president of the board of directors, and Gerald's best friend, Stephen Kuhn, is the treasurer. My granddaughter, who was so instrumental in helping Gerald with the publication of *Crisis 2038* in his last days, now manages the Amazon and Audible accounts. Jane is a film editor and she created three two-minute videos from an almost two-hour-long interview that Gerald did in 2017. From the interview, she picked three topics and coupled his in-person discussions with illustrative animation. If you go to the fund's website, https://fundforhumanity.org/universal-basic-income-discussions-with-gerald-huff/, you will meet Gerald and hear him discuss 1) the foundation of UBI, 2) automation in the circular economy, and 3) adjusting our economy.

Having lined up the infrastructure for the fund, I flew to New York in May 2019, where I met with Andrew Yang. His campaign office was in a nondescript building and had a staff of eight people, none of whom was older than thirty-five, a rather startling fact. Andrew's campaign was very much a young people's campaign, and part of the goal of the fund is to mobilize the next generation to agitate for UBI at the national level.

In general, proponents of UBI tend to be younger people, many academics being men and a preponderance of activists and organizers being women. It seems that older people are loath to let go of the convictions that were true at an earlier time: the power and accessibility of the American Dream, the view that America is a democracy, and the belief that we live in a meritocracy. Older people are also less likely to acknowledge the challenges of technological unemployment and the forthcoming loss of jobs.

Rick introduced me to Rob Johnson, the president of the Institute for New Economic Thinking, with whom I established an immediate connection. I shared my life story with Rob, which led me to write this autobiography. I've found that telling the story of my extraordinary circumstances evokes a response in people that goes beyond casual meetings of the mind. As you will see later, my story apparently had the same effect on Rob.

I also had an opportunity to have dinner with one of Gerald's high school friends who had flown to California for his celebration of life. I am respecting his wish for anonymity, but suffice it to say that this man holds a very prominent position in the international world of marketing and branding. As we discussed how he could contribute to the fund, he proposed that his West Coast affiliates create and distribute a thirty-second spot about UBI on a pro bono basis. That couldn't have been a better fit for my goals, and I met with his colleagues in San Francisco in September 2019.

My first meeting with the CEOs of this prominent company reflected the status of UBI in 2019. They had vaguely heard of UBI, but I had to explain it as best I could in the one-hour time slot allotted for our meeting. They asked me that famous question "What would success look like?" and I could only answer that the thirty-second spot should raise awareness of the concept. Thus, I embarked on a very exciting learning experience. I had no idea of the workings of the advertising world other than what I had gleaned from assiduously watching the TV series *Mad Men*.

A team of five people began by creating a template that framed three different scenarios about UBI as well as identifying the demographic we'd target. They did market research and, in consultation with me, narrowed the narrative down to three messages and two audience clusters. By January 2020, we had come up with a solid plan. Then, the pandemic struck. By mid-March, California was in lockdown.

CHAPTER 25

Not only was 2020 a challenge for me as it was for everyone else, but I also experienced a very frightening experience unrelated to COVID-19. Just as the lockdown began and hospitals imposed pandemic-related restrictions, I had a dramatic episode of renal failure. Over a period of two days, I couldn't urinate, my eyes became puffy, I had diarrhea, and I felt nauseated. My primary care physician recommended that I go to the emergency room. Michèle and I, worried about the possibly chaotic intake process, called an ambulance to take me there. When I arrived, my creatinine level was 5.6, whereas the normal number for a woman is between 0.5 and 1.0. I was immediately admitted to a non-COVID-19 geriatric floor and put in a private room, where all efforts were made to stimulate urination. A port was inserted in my neck in case I needed dialysis, and the possibility of it becoming a lifelong necessity loomed large.

After six days, my creatinine level was down to 1.5, and I was released with a walker and returned home. An aide came to help me with my first shower and a therapist walked me through a series of mild exercises. This episode gave me a foretaste of what old age looks like, the indignities it imposes, and the challenges it presents.

Then in June, just before my birthday, my creatinine level shot up to 4.2, and this time the five-day hospital stay involved a PET scan, which revealed that I had chronic lymphocytic leukemia. CLL is a blood cancer that has some seventy different types of expression, mine being at the lower level of concern. My doctors speculated, but could not confirm, because they hadn't previously encountered a case like mine, that my kidneys could not cope with the cells that CLL was generating and, thus, started to shut down. After five days, my creatinine level went down to 1.3 and I was discharged with the additional care of an oncologist. The doctors decided that I should start chemotherapy with four infusions administered one week apart. My oncologist informed me that, were it not for the peculiar reaction of my kidneys, my CLL condition wouldn't have required any intervention.

The first infusion was closely supervised to ascertain the appropriate dosage. While I was ensconced in a recliner in a private space with a few nurses in attendance, the drip started, and after a few minutes, an incredible pain radiated around my back and my stomach, so searing that I started to scream and sob uncontrollably. I have a high tolerance of pain (in 1985, I walked around with a torn rotator cuff for eighteen months), but this was indescribable. I begged for relief, but the nursing station was not prepared for this reaction and had to get permission to administer morphine, which took twenty minutes—the longest twenty minutes I have ever experienced.

Unfortunately, the four infusions did not do the trick, because in the last week of October, I had to go back to the hospital with a 2.6 creatinine level, the third time in 2020 that I had to spend five or more days in the hospital. At that point,

I called in two experts from UCSF for second opinions, and all four doctors agreed that I should start treatment with a drug called Imbruvica. This drug is only partially covered by insurance, private or Medicare, and costs $700 a month. I'm grateful that I can afford the cost and it seems to have done the trick, but the price tag underscores how callous our health-care system is.

Imbruvica has been around for a long time, and I'm sure its manufacturers have earned back their investment. But this lifesaving medicine and many others such as insulin are cash cows for patent holders. Instead of lowering their prices in the same way manufacturers have lowered prices on products such as TV sets, the patent holders have increased the price. People can survive without TV sets but not without essential medications. But that doesn't matter in our system, where no allowances are made for those who have low income. People should not have to decide between paying the rent, putting food on the table, or paying for their medications. This is especially true for older people who live on fixed incomes and have seen interest rates fall to zero. Medicare Part D covers drugs but only generic ones, not the ones still protected by patents.

The argument that if it weren't for these inflated profits, Big Pharma would not develop new and innovative drugs, is hogwash. Why else would they be in business? Many groundbreaking drugs have been invented by lean start-ups that are then bought out by big companies who ultimately reap the profits or shelve the product if it would compete more cheaply with one of their existing drugs. I was shocked to learn that four of the largest drug companies spend twice as much on marketing as they do on research and development. Not to mention that the average profit margin of pharmaceuticals is typically more than twice that of other non-pharmaceutical companies of the same size.

Other than living with CLL, I am in good physical shape. Every day, I spend thirty minutes on my stationary bike and take a walk for forty-five minutes to an hour. Aside from the annoying aches and pains that come with age, I am quite healthy. I attribute my health not only to physical exercise and my very disciplined diet (I don't eat junk food, drink soda, or smoke, and I don't drink except socially), but also to the fact that I keep myself thoroughly engaged. My work in promoting UBI gives me a reason to get up every morning and look forward to the day. I strongly recommend espousing a cause and committing to it no matter your age. It will keep you young.

CHAPTER 26

During my stays at the hospital, I took along my iPad, my cell phone, and my chargers and continued to work on the ad campaign for the fund. I did not interrupt my work with the team at the advertising agency. When they overshot their allotted pro bono budget, they reached out to their international colleagues for volunteers to help with the project. Six people volunteered, two from overseas. The team was astounded. Normally these sorts of appeals generate only one or two interested parties.

We agreed upon the message and a target audience in September 2020, all while working remotely. The team then developed a thirty-second ad and convinced one of the firms they worked with to survey eight hundred people for their reaction to the ad, pro bono. Here again, the team went above and beyond, marshaling elements of a successful campaign far beyond my budget. The survey reflected a 60 percent approval of the ad, far above the usual results. The comment I liked best was "The ad is stirring. I could see it causing a revolt." Of course, that's exactly what I'm after.

After production, the marketing team took over. They lined up ten mainstream media outlets, including Viacom, BuzzFeed, and the *Wall Street Journal* Online, to run the thirty-second video as a public service announcement, free of cost. The campaign ran from January 14 to February 28, 2021, and the ad garnered 7,129,884 impressions, with 60 percent viewing it fully. In several instances, the video completion rate was two to three times higher than the platforms' benchmarks.

The campaign was a huge success at almost no cost to the fund (I paid only $10,000 for production expenses provided by third parties). The ad reached thousands of people not necessarily familiar with UBI. It played on the theme that since we all contribute to the economy in myriad ways, we all should reap the benefits—the very same message Gerald conveyed in his book.

What I found amazing about the experience is that so many people who didn't know me or anything about the Gerald Huff Fund for Humanity were willing to give their time and talent with no remuneration. This is a testament to the power of the idea of UBI and my compelling story. Not only was the ad a success, but it also epitomized the notion that we can achieve so much when we collaborate. It is in our DNA to work together. We wouldn't have survived as a species if it wasn't.

Earlier, in June 2019, Scott Santens had introduced me to an amazing woman, Stacey Rutland, who had been very involved in Andrew Yang's campaign. She was working to put together an event dubbed the Basic Income March to promote UBI and build on the momentum from Andrew's campaign. Marches would take place all over the world, but Stacey's primary focus was on the New York City march because the idea came from two New Yorkers, Diane Pagen and James Felton Keith. Stacey was in desperate need of financial support for the march. Up to that time, volunteers had planned all aspects of the worldwide march. With the infusion of a mere $25,000 from the fund, the march took place in October 2019, in thirteen countries and thirty cities—a huge success.

I was also instrumental in supporting the San Francisco Basic Income March on October 27, 2019. It was the lead-in for a Yang rally, and it drew some three hundred people. We gathered at the Civic Center Plaza, where I was one of the speakers, and then we marched down Market Street and back. My family joined me in this exhilarating experience. I marched in the front row, carrying the event's banner, and you can still see me in the archived pictures on the internet. At one point, I was too tired to continue holding up the banner, so Michèle took over, and the picture of her shouting a slogan also lives on the internet. The most stirring slogan for me was "This is what democracy looks like."

In 2020, due to COVID-19, the activists took part in car and bike parades, but in 2021, on September 25, we held the third annual Basic Income March in Mountain View. We had an amazing lineup of speakers, including Andrew Yang, Natalie Foster, and Martin Ford, the author of the seminal 2009 book *The Lights in the Tunnel: Automation, Accelerating Technology and the Economy of the Future.*

I took the stage and was introduced as the founder and president of the Gerald Huff Fund for Humanity and as the sponsor of the nationwide march. While introducing California State Senator Dave Cortese, I told the crowd that I was eighty-five years old, intending to make the point that for the first time ever, I believed UBI would be implemented within my lifetime. After Senator Cortese made it clear that California and his legislation are in the vanguard of making UBI a federal reality, Andrew Yang took the stage. Halfway through his speech, he stopped to describe his relationship with Gerald and how shocked he was when he learned of his passing. He turned to me and choked up as he acknowledged that he had no idea what it feels like to lose a child but that the work I am doing in Gerald's name will undoubtedly help change the world.

One of the speakers, Kevin Dublin, the recipient of the basic income pilot run by the Yerba Buena Center for the Arts, whom you met earlier, made an impassioned case for the moral and philosophical need for universal basic income. He said:

> We have to believe that a guaranteed minimum income isn't radical. . . . It isn't radical for each citizen to have enough to eat or a financial safety net; it isn't radical for each citizen to have the financial freedom to fail: to start a business or create culture; it isn't radical for each citizen to be able to take care of their family or their community and still feel valued. It isn't radical to know we need more and DEMAND IT. When we get a universal basic income, and we will get it, it's a starting point. We all know from the first time our four-or-so-year-old hands draw circles in the sand, or with chalk on a sidewalk, or with a large pencil on paper, that each circle begins with a starting point. Each starting point can become a revolution.

Given the success of the first Basic Income March in 2019, Stacey started a grassroots organization, Income Movement, to capitalize on the burgeoning interest in UBI. A master at organizing and operations, she combines her passion for the cause with the expertise to make things happen. Since its inception, I have been a major funder of Income Movement. I view it as the public-facing arm of the fund and I'm a proud member of its board.

History has taught me that to make policy change, aside from funding, we need to demonstrate demand for the cause. We need to mobilize a large number of people to convince the powers that be to implement change. It can take a long time to reach a tipping point, and the proponents of a cause must be patient and keep on pushing. It took women seventy years to get the vote and it took gay people fifty years to be able to marry.

As an example of the power in numbers, I like to cite the Townsend Clubs, founded in 1933 by Dr. Francis E. Townsend, the author of the Townsend Plan. Within two years, over 3,400 Townsend Clubs operated across the country and galvanized some five million people to put pressure on Congress to provide support for people over the age of sixty during the desperate days of the Great Depression. Frances Perkins, President Franklin D. Roosevelt's secretary of labor, wrote in her memoir that Roosevelt told her, "The Congress can't stand the pressure of the Townsend Plan unless we are studying social security, a solid plan which will give some assurance to old people of systematic assistance upon retirement."

I continue to provide financial support for Income Movement in an aim to mobilize the proponents of UBI and encourage them to demand that the prosperity they help create redounds to their benefit as well. Income Movement gives people an opportunity to take action. It's not enough to talk the talk; we must walk the walk, and Income Movement provides many different options for participation.

I truly believe that small contributions can make a big difference. Another investment the Fund for Humanity made was to professionalize the annual North American Basic Income Guarantee (NABIG) Congress. The group had been meeting annually, alternating locations between the US and Canada, and drawing some 150 people to hear academics and other proponents of UBI present papers for discussion. The meetings were entirely run by volunteers with a very small budget. For the nineteenth NABIG Congress, I made a $15,000 grant to Stacey's Income Movement, and she shaped it into a successful virtual meeting that drew 650 people. It featured very well-received sessions and established a new benchmark for the event. The event was free, but attendees were encouraged to contribute whatever they could, and almost $10,000 was raised as a result.

Inspired by the experience I had with the vision document I helped produce for Education Reimagined, I decided to launch another initiative. My original purpose was to convene a group of people to discuss UBI and to collaborate in the creation of a document that would provide a definitive goal for the movement as a whole. I hired the Consensus Building Institute (CBI), the outstanding group that had guided the Education Reimagined project, to explore the possibility of creating such a document. The modus operandi of CBI is to bring together a group of disparate people to discuss a topic about which there is no consensus and then to build consensus. Unfortunately, the initiative was not viable—first, because it presupposed that proponents are in agreement on the ultimate goal of UBI, and second, because in the small universe of UBI proponents and opponents, we couldn't get enough response for the project to move forward.

It was a disappointment, but I had already invested in the project, so the facilitators and I set about finding a different approach. I have always believed that it is a mistake to fall in love with an idea and refuse to move on when it becomes obvious that it's not viable. Shifting gears is how you exercise control even when it requires letting go. In fact, as I found with Education Reimagined, letting go helped me eventually accomplish what I had set my mind to, even though I had to modify my goal to adapt to the circumstances.

We decided to focus on exploring the viability of a convening in which we'd develop a vision for society twenty years in the future. We set out to approach leaders in the fields of economics, social justice, business, academics, and philanthropy. I thought UC Berkeley would be a good venue for the convening because the university hosted the Haas Institute for a Fair and Inclusive Society, since then renamed the Othering and Belonging Institute. To add credibility to the project, given how little was known about the Gerald Huff Fund for Humanity at that time, I decided to enlist john powell [*sic*], whose impeccable credentials include professor of law at UC Berkeley, professor of African American studies and ethnic studies, Robert D. Haas Chancellor's Chair in Equity and Inclusion, and director of the Othering and Belonging Institute.

Wendy Ake, a delightful young colleague of john's, scheduled an introductory telephone call for us. He has a very busy schedule, so I had to make myself available whenever it worked for him. We had the call when I was on a school visit during an iNACOL conference. I excused myself from the tour and spoke with john for an hour, at the end of which he agreed to be the co-convener. I can't tell you how important, exciting, and yes, surprising, that was. After all, john is an icon in the social justice movement, and we have never met in person. Since then, john and I, coming from entirely different backgrounds and life experiences, have found again and again that we are aligned in our mission.

We had our notable roster finalized in May 2020, and CBI put together a technologically impressive series of Zoom calls that featured extremely well-run sessions and breakout rooms, allowing participants to express their opinions and discuss their objections in a civilized and very productive manner. At the end of each meeting, CBI wrote up a synopsis of the discussions. They shared that document with the participants, who then could comment and make suggestions. The revised document became the starting point for the next meeting. This process was repeated six times to create the final document.

The pandemic prevented us from meeting in person and I missed the camaraderie of getting together, but because of the commitment of the participants, the end product we created is quite a spectacular document. Titled "Vision and Foundations for a Better Society: Automation, Opportunity, and Belonging," it is so impressive that one of our most distinguished participants, Rob Johnson, who is president of the Institute for New Economic Thinking and as such, has a big megaphone, offered to promote the document. He committed to doing a series of interviews, both audio and video, on YouTube. He started the series with an interview with john powell and me, recorded in our respective homes.

Rob introduced john and me and asked me to speak about how and why I reached out to john. I explained that the project needed his credentials and his gravitas to lend it credibility. Rob then asked john the same question and to my astonishment, this was his answer: "And so, as they say, I was waiting for years to be in that conversation with Gisèle. So, when it finally happened, I was delighted. And I think the vision that she brought to this was just so important not just for this project, but for the whole country, if not the whole world." I couldn't believe my ears. It dawned on me that somehow, I had a greater reach than I imagined. It reminded me of what

President Harry S. Truman once said: "It is amazing what you can accomplish if you do not care who gets the credit."

The document lays out what the signatories envision that society ought to be in a generation, and the introduction reads:

> Because technology, social, economic, and political conditions are evolving rapidly, and because further disruptive change seems inevitable, the Vision and Foundations do not include detailed policy prescriptions or institutional strategies for the next several years, nor do we propose a roadmap for establishing the foundations for the vision. Rather, we offer a "North Star" of principles, rights, and institutions to guide the direction of social change. Our ambition is that activists, thinkers, civic, and political and business leaders read and respond to the Vision and Foundations as a way to test their own beliefs about what kind of society we should be striving to create for the next generation. It is meant as a conversation starter, a constructive provocation, and an encouragement for those who seek a transformation in our values and institutions to achieve a society where all Americans experience equal value, participation, and belonging.

The document sets a new baseline for individuals and society. People are like snowflakes; no two of them are exactly alike. A polity that recognizes and neutralizes differences is the next step in human evolution. The document also underscores that, although individuals make decisions all the time, these decisions are not the result of unfettered free will;

humans are heavily influenced by the circumstances in which they find themselves. Acknowledging that, the document goes on to outline the four elements that would comprise the most responsive environment: enabling technology, communities of belonging, embraced identities, and liberatory education. A word here about the word *liberatory.* Liberating education is one that removes the shackles of traditional schooling and enables learners to take control of their own learning, much as I described in previous chapters. Liberatory education is deeper and wider because it includes an awareness of the paradigms in which we find ourselves and an actionable pathway to freeing ourselves from them.

For me, the most powerful part of the vision document is the part about communities of belonging. I attribute a great deal of the divisions that rend our country to the fact that many Americans feel that they don't belong—in particular, marginalized communities excluded since the country was founded and people in rural communities who have seen the Fourth Industrial Revolution destroy their livelihoods and their place in the world. If your identity is tied to a job and it disappears, who are you? At the core of the Vision and Foundations document is this phrase: "Respect for intrinsic human dignity [is] not contingent on job, income, wealth, or identity." You can access the document here: https://socialcontract.fundforhumanity.org/.

I also invested in the UBI Calculator, a website where you can enter information about your income and the size of your family to find out how UBI would affect you, using nine separate scenarios. These scenarios posit different ways of paying for UBI and the different outcomes.

One of the most meaningful pilots I participated in was a UBI pilot for youth transitioning out of the foster care system in Santa Clara County. rick keating [*sic*] introduced me to then supervisor Cortese, and over lunch we came up with the idea. At the hearing about its implementation, I offered to fund a research paper to speed the process along. The committee chair welcomed the offer, commenting that this was very unusual as most organizations seek funds rather than donate them. The Board of Supervisors subsequently voted unanimously to fund the project, the first time in this century when the funding for the cash transfer to the participants of the pilot was publicly rather than privately funded. Cortese successfully ran for the California Senate and has continued championing UBI, proposing a law to take the program statewide, which was very well received by his colleagues. At almost every opportunity, Cortese gives me much more credit than I deserve. In that respect, he is an unusual politician and I very much admire his humility.

Senator Cortese's integrity and graciousness are especially noteworthy at a time when our elected officials in Congress have lost sight of their responsibilities to their constituents. They pay much more heed to their donors, given that in the House of Representatives they must run for election every two years. Fundraising is a very time-consuming activity, one that takes time away from legislating. In my view, we're not governed by the people we elect; instead we're governed by the pack of young, underpaid congressional staff members who help write the laws (in many cases alongside the lobbyists whose clients have a stake in those laws). Between posturing for the media and making incessant calls to donors, our representatives are in a perpetual reelection campaign. No wonder we have such gridlock in Washington, DC, above and beyond the corrosive partisanship that eats away at our republic.

I find even more disturbing the glaring flaws in our system. The number of members in the House of Representatives was fixed at 435 in 1913, when the population of the United

States was 97.22 million. It was made permanent in 1929. As of 2019, the population was 328.22 million, over three times greater than the population in 1913. Similarly, in the Senate, every state continues to get two senators, regardless of its population. In Wyoming two senators represent 578,759 people, while in California, two senators represent an astounding 39.51 million people. "One person, one vote" and the perception that we are a republic are demonstrably, mathematically false.

As of February 2021, Congress's approval rating is 28 percent, but in the 2020 election, 92 percent of incumbents returned to office. Out of the 435 congressional districts, 359 are considered safe, meaning they are gerrymandered in such a way, both by Democrats and Republicans, that winning the primary is tantamount to winning the seat. That means that the small percentage of people who vote in primaries (usually people with the most extreme ideologies on either side of the political divide) decide who governs. In a safe district, the incumbent doesn't need to make hard decisions and is, in fact, incentivized not to do so, because they are practically assured of reelection. They spend more than half their time fundraising either for themselves or for their colleagues, and they avoid taking positions for the commonweal that their constituents may consider radical. The illusion that we can hold our representatives accountable is just that, an illusion.

Add to this the fact that our senators are growing more and more out of touch with their constituents. The average age of senators at the start of 2021 was 64.3 years, but out of the one hundred members, only one is under forty, while twenty-three are in their seventies. And let's not forget Senator Dianne Feinstein, eighty-eight; Senator Richard Shelby, eighty-seven; Senator James Inhofe, eighty-six; Senator Pat Leahy, eighty-one; and Senator Charles Grassley, eighty-eight. Grassley will run for his ninth term at the end of which he will be ninety-four years old. There's something to be said for the advantage of experience, but serving into your nineties is taking things too far. These senators lived a significant portion of their lives in an America entirely different from the one we live in now. Whatever experience they bring is far outweighed by their inability to relate to the constituents they ostensibly represent. Given that people now live much longer, and that many institutions impose age limits on their practitioners, I would like to see the same sort of limits on Congress, the presidency, and the Supreme Court.

The institutions that held us in good stead for nearly 250 years are no longer capable of delivering adequate solutions for today's problems. Running our country has become so complex that Americans have become jaded and impatient. Mind you, no one should expect perfection, but now, thanks to social media, every failure is amplified and worried like an abscessed tooth, while successes are rarely mentioned. Add the stress of the pandemic and it's no wonder we walk around in perpetual outrage with nary a solution in sight. Think about the presidency. How can one woman or man handle the challenges of foreign relations and domestic needs while also acting as commander in chief, consoler in chief, and manager of the bully pulpit? It's a three-person job: domestic affairs, foreign affairs, and communicator in chief. Sadly, the odds of restructuring the presidency are as good as the odds of eliminating the Electoral College or increasing the number of Supreme Court justices.

But I haven't given up hope. Despite the disastrous political situation, I think Gerald would be amazed at the momentum UBI has gained in the few years since his death. Pre-pandemic, proponents focused on UBI's moral and philosophical aspects with less emphasis on ways to pay for it. Now that we've seen how stimulus checks and the Child Tax Credit have had positive effects on the economy, the national conversation has shifted to addressing the practical need for direct cash payments. To survive as a nation, we need to rewrite our social contract so that it covers all of us, not just the ruling elites. This is my most passionate wish.

As long as time permits, I will continue to funnel my energy into UBI. Unfortunately, my work has slowed a bit in recent months. On September 21, Michèle called and asked if I would like her to come into the city and take a walk. This was somewhat unusual because we normally see each other on the weekend, but I agreed. She let herself in with her key as I finished a Zoom call. She sat down on the sofa, said she had something to tell me, and as I faced her, she took my hands and pulled me over closer to her. She told me not to freak out and announced that she had been diagnosed with early-stage breast cancer. I almost fainted. I felt my eyes roll back in my head and couldn't catch my breath. It took several minutes for me to hear her repeating over and over that it was three small lumps, not the same as Gerald's cancer, and rattling off names of people we know who have survived breast cancer.

On October 11, Michèle underwent a double mastectomy, even though only one breast was affected. She couldn't bear the thought of undergoing the radiation and chemotherapy required after a lumpectomy, and she didn't want to spend the rest of her life worrying whether the other breast would become cancerous. I agreed with her decision. She has recovered remarkably well. When I hugged her for the first time post-surgery, I felt the absence of her breasts, but she is a strong person who is very comfortable in her skin. I know she will adjust without any problem.

As you now know, my life has been an endless series of challenges, and at the age of eighty-six, I anticipate it will continue to be. I have developed a very thick skin and I put a premium on the value of life. For me, it has always been an either-or proposition: either you find a way to deal with what fate has dealt you and make the best of it, or you decide to give up. For me, there is no middle ground.

Every day, as I work at promoting Gerald's vision, I feel that he is still with me. He was so perceptive and off-the-charts smart. What I miss most of all, aside from the hugs (at six feet, one inch tall, he was a world-class, all-embracing hugger), was his ability to keep me in check. As you may have noticed, I tend to pontificate, and when I took off on flights of hyperbole, he would wait for the right moment to say "But Mom . . ." and effectively put a pin in my oratorial balloon. He was the only person in the world who could do that.

Recently my grandson, Paul, stopped by for dinner. After Gerald's death, he remained in the Bay Area and was accepted into Hastings Law School. He will graduate this year. The heart-wrenching experience of losing his father, to whom he was very attached, transformed him and motivated him to find a purpose in life. He was always a very big proponent of social justice. His first BFF was his Black neighbor, and when he was in preschool, he colored himself brown in his self-portrait.

At the time of our dinner Paul had an externship with Open Door Legal, whose motto is "The law belongs to all of us." The externship was right up his alley, having graduated summa cum laude in sociology from UC Santa Barbara. He took me in his arms and gave me a big hug, knowing full well how much I missed his father's embraces. Over wine, we talked about his work helping low-income people who don't have access to lawyers challenge the inequities they encounter.

I was thrilled at his enthusiasm and the way he articulated his feelings and reactions because ten years earlier, he was a lost soul looking for purpose in life, much to the despair of his father. In our conversation, I heard echoes of conversations I had with Gerald, and I realized with pride and awe that Paul is the last of the men I loved.

I could have given up after the tragedy of Gerald's death. But instead, it spurred me on to do things I could never have foreseen, which is pretty much the story of my life. As I told Gerald, I am a survivor because life is the most precious of all things, and what you do with it is the reason you are living it.

EPILOGUE

I still love America, but in the year 2022, I find the state of our nation devastating. I'm horrified by the upsurge in racism and anti-Semitism in recent years and dread what it will inevitably lead to if left unchecked. Having survived the draconian regime of the German occupation of France, I've always pushed back against the cavalier attitude of Americans who argue that such a thing could never happen here. It is happening here, not through the invasion of a foreign power (although we can see fingerprints of overseas trolls interfering with our elections all over the internet), but through the implosion of the norms that have sustained our democracy for 246 years.

For someone whose mantra is "Never Forget" and who reacts viscerally to anti-Semitism, the current situation is terrifying. What particularly concerns me is the apparent helplessness of governmental authorities, the indifference of those not affected, and the virulence of those who perpetuate the violence. I cannot describe the horror I felt when I watched clips of the march of the Nazis in Charlottesville, Virginia, on August 11 and 12, 2017, where they chanted "Jews will not replace us," and "blood and soil," echoing slogans heard in Germany some eighty years ago. I couldn't believe my eyes as I watched the mostly young white men carrying tiki torches, coursing through the streets of Charlottesville, not far from the seat of our democracy in Washington, DC.

Although I've written this book to convey the urgent need to transform the way our children learn and the way our economy works, the greatest threat to our way of life and the future of our children is the resurgence and normalization of anti-Semitism and racism. Hitler and his minions took their cue from the Jim Crow playbook and amplified it by killing thirteen million people in an attempt to establish an Aryan hegemony. This may seem like a remote historical factoid to you, not much more relevant than the barbarism of the Middle Ages, but take it from one who lived through the Holocaust, we are a hairbreadth away from chaos and annihilation. After the Second World War ended, Protestant pastor Martin Niemöller wrote this moving passage about being a German at the onset of the Hitler regime:

> First they came for the socialists, and I did not
> speak out—because I was not a socialist.
>
> Then they came for the trade unionists, and I
> did not speak out—because I was not a trade
> unionist. Then they came for the Jews, and I
> did not speak out—because I was not a Jew.

> Then they came for me—and there was no
> one left to speak for me.

It is my greatest wish that we gather the courage to speak out before it's too late.

ACKNOWLEDGMENTS

In writing the story of my life, I want to thank all the people I met along the way who had an impact on the person I have become, many of whom are mentioned in the book. This memoir was a labor of love, and it is my pleasure to acknowledge those who made specific contributions.

My daughter, Michèle Huff, skillfully edited the first draft and gave me the confidence to undertake the enormous project of distilling eighty-six years of life into one book. I'm also grateful to my granddaughter, Jane Huff, and my friends Sue Toigo and Bill Buster, who read early drafts and provided feedback as well as confirmation of the value of my project. As the work progressed, I called on two former colleagues and dear friends for their expertise. Scott Ellis meticulously removed and added commas, but most importantly he challenged ideas and turns of phrase, much to the benefit of the book. Michael Horn not only added his comments and suggestions but introduced me to the world's best editor, Jodi Warshaw.

In what must be the fastest turnaround in the history of book editing, Jodi delivered the final version of the book in fourteen days. As you can tell, she did not sacrifice quality for speed, and she captured and maintained my voice throughout. In addition to that, she is a warm, caring person and it has been my privilege to share this endeavor with her.

Finally, I want to acknowledge the masterful work of Girl

Friday Productions. In a world where book publishing has been transformed, my team added the professionalism and commitment that used to be provided by traditional book publishers, and this book is a product of their expertise.

CREDITS

Definition of blended learning courtesy of Michael Horn.

Excerpts from the Convergence vision courtesy of the author.

Excerpt by Martin Friedman from *Capitalism and Freedom* (University of Chicago Press, 2003).

Excerpt by Martin Luther King, Jr., from *Where Do We Go from Here: Chaos or Community?* (King Legacy, 2010).

Quote from Kevin Dublin used with his permission.

"The Labor Content Fallacy" by Gerald Huff reproduced courtesy of Dr. Judith Bliss.

Quote by Andrew Yang from *Crisis 2038* by Gerald Huff (BookBaby, 2018) courtesy of Dr. Judith Bliss.

Quote by Scott Santens from *Crisis 2038* by Gerald Huff (BookBaby, 2018) courtesy of Dr. Judith Bliss.

Quote from David Lau used with his permission.

Excerpt from *Crisis 2038* by Gerald Huff (BookBaby, 2018) courtesy of Dr. Judith Bliss.

Extract from Scott Santens's eulogy of Gerald Huff used with his permission.

Excerpt by Frances Perkins from *The Roosevelt I Knew* by Frances Perkins (Penguin, 2011).

Quote from john powell from "On Developing a Vision for a Better Society," *Economics and Beyond* (Institute for New Economic Thinking, 2021) courtesy of Rob Johnson.

Excerpts from "Vision and Foundations for a Better Society:

Automation, Opportunity, and Belonging" by the Gerald Huff Fund for Humanity (2021) courtesy of the author.

Excerpt by Martin Niemöller from *Martin Niemöller: 1892–1984* by James Bentley (Free Press, 1984).

ABOUT THE AUTHOR

Gisèle Huff was born in 1936 in Paris to working-class Russian Jewish immigrants. She moved to the US when she was eleven and went on to earn a PhD in political science from Columbia University. For more than two decades, Gisèle served as the executive director of the Jaquelin Hume Foundation, which invested in nonprofit, national organizations that worked on transforming K–12 education. She received the Thomas A. Roe Award and the iNACOL Huff Lifetime Achievement Award. She is deeply involved in raising awareness about technological unemployment and promoting universal basic income, the legacy of her late son. She is the founder of the Gerald Huff Fund for Humanity. She lives in San Francisco, California. This is her first book.

CPSIA information can be obtained
at www.ICGtesting.com
Printed in the USA
LVHW020256151122
733111LV00004B/535